the chick commentary continues...

"No way can you read all these true tales of youthful escapades and matronly misdemeanors—or sense the sisterly spirit that informed them—without wanting to get down with your gal pals right this very minute. Fresh, fun, and non-phallocentric without making a big deal about it, *It's a Chick Thing* depicts female friendship at its finest."

—Autumn Stephens, author of *Wild Women, Drama Queens,* and several other books in The Wild Women genre

"Every one of my super-chick, super-siSTAR, goddess girlfriends is going to get a copy of this book as a grand and glorious 'Thank You' for lighting up my life with their wildness, wisdom, and raging faith in all things beautiful."

—Margie Lapanja, author of *Goddess in the Kitchen* and *The Goddess' Guide to Love*

"'Über-chicks' Ame and Emily have long been two of my personal sheroes for their feisty ferocity. This book unleashes enough 'chick power' to save the world!"

—Varla Ventura, author of *Sheroes: Bold, Brash and Absolutely Unabashed Superwomen*

"Full of fun and female frolic. Read it with your best friend and then cut loose."

—Alicia Alvrez, author of *The Ladies' Room Reader*

to: _____

from: _____

"Friends are the family we choose for ourselves."

—Edna Buchanan

it's a Chick Thing

it's a Chick Thing

CElebratinG *the* Wild SIde *of* WOmen's FrIendship

edited by *Ame Mahler Beanland and Emily Miles Terry*

foreword by *Jill Conner Browne*
author of *The Sweet Potato Queens' Book of Love*

BARNES & NOBLE BOOKS

NEW YORK

Published by MJF Books
Fine Communications
322 Eighth Avenue
New York, NY 10001

It's a Chick Thing
Library of Congress Control Number 2001090532
ISBN 1-56731-461-9
Copyright © 2000 Ame Mahler Beanland and Emily Miles Terry

This edition published by arrangement with Conari Press.
Cover and book design: Ame Beanland
Illustrations: Martha Newton Furman Design and Illustration
cover photo: Vintage Superstock
chapter openers: Archive Photo

Manufactured in the United States of America on acid-free paper
MJF Books and the MJF colophon are trademarks of Fine Creative Media, Inc.

DH   11   10   9   8   7   6   5   4   3

This book is dedicated to all our chick buddies, gal pals, sister-friends, and partners in crime for their endless support through Barbies, braces, bell-bottoms, big hair, and bad boyfriends. You are cherished.

conTents

foreword

Every word in this book is true. I only say that for the men who read it—every woman who reads it will know its truth instinctively. We could swear it was all made up and women would know better.

What we as Sweet Potato Queens (of whom I am the mainmost boss) have discovered—and what you are going to experience between the covers of this book—is the power of play, the magical, healing, and restorative powers of play. We never outgrow our need for it. I don't believe that we quit playing because we got too old. Rather, I believe that we get old, and seem older still, because we quit playing. The good news is, it's never too late.

I bear witness to this phenomenon every St. Patrick's Day, when legions of women from across the country converge upon my hometown of Jackson, Mississippi, for that sole purpose—just to play. The lot of them—and lord, there are a *lot* of them—take time off work, buy plane tickets, make hotel reservations, construct *costumes*, and come all the way to Jackson, Mississippi, to play. They dress up as the Queen of Whatever They Choose and they march in the St. Patrick's Day parade—and every single one of them say it is the most fun they have ever had in their lives and they do not think they can *live* until next year, when they can do it . . . again.

The stories in this book may appear to be merely fun and frolic— as if that wouldn't be enough—but there's truly a higher purpose to it all. It represents the women's movement come full circle. We've fought and struggled for attention and equality, and in our efforts to be taken seriously we've taken ourselves too seriously at times. And although there is still much work to be done to level the playing field, we are finally able to revel in our femininity and celebrate our connections with other women. We are able to risk and play and just be ourselves. That's a glorious thing.

A man said to a group of us women one day that listening to us made him long for what he did not believe in: that another person could really understand what one is about. It got very quiet and we looked at him in utter disbelief and sympathy bordering on outright pity. "Bless your heart," someone surely said to him, with a loving pat.

Our understanding of each other seems to be complete in utero—we just have the rest of our lives to enjoy it. It's a Chick Thing—thank God!

—JILL CONNER BROWNE, THE Sweet Potato Queen and author of *The Sweet Potato Queens' Book of Love*

"God, I love a tiara."

—Jill Conner Browne

the cHick mAnifestO

The creation of this book has generated a lot of discussion about the clumsy, fun, silly, sometimes downright insulting ways people attempt to give name to our essence, our spirit, as women—chick, girlfriend, babe, gal, broad, sister, dame, feminist. Some were coined within our own ranks, others by men; some we embrace or tolerate, others we reject outright.

Most of us spurn rigid labels. One day we might choose to be our "chick" persona—wearing a hot red lipstick and ferociously high heels; the next day we might choose to be "woooman" and wear a crisp white blouse with khaki pants. One day we might want to smoke a cigar and blurt out Dorothy Parker witticisms at an office party, the next day we're putting on our scarf pin and sitting down to high tea at a stuffy hotel with Aunt Martha. We're unapologetic about our feminine and our feminist sides and how we choose to manifest and celebrate them. Let's put it this way—some of us want to wear lipstick to the bra burning. Don't try to define us—we have attitude and an inalienable right to be unpredictable, enigmatic, and female.

Our good friends, our girlfriends, let us do this. That is what this book is about—how our girlfriends allow and encourage us to expand our boundaries, defy definition, and do it all while simultaneously comfortably residing within our own skins.

The stories in this book are meant to amuse and entertain, but they also explore themes of growth, commitment, loss, self-identity, and memory. What we do in the name of adventure, thrill-seeking and sport can sometimes mask its higher purpose in the eyes of the uninitiated—that of connection, bonding, and celebration. This book is a testament to the ways that friendship forms and influences our lives as women—our minds, our bodies, our emotions—*and* our lipstick color.

We celebrate all sides of women's friendships—from the merciless jokes we play on men in bars to how we encourage each other in the workplace and offer one another the unflagging support that only girlfriends can deliver. So next time you feel like wrapping your head in a scarf ala *Thelma and Louise* or belting out your favorite girl's-night anthem, succumb. And to your critics deliver a sassy, "It's a chick thing," and leave it at that.

—Ame Mahler Beanland and Emily Miles Terry

"It's life, Sidda.
You just climb on the beast and ride."

—Vivi Abbot, in *Divine Secrets of the Ya-Ya Sisterhood,*
by Rebecca Wells

"Ouiser could never stay mad at me.
She worships the quicksand
I walk on."

—Clarice in *Steel Magnolias*

1

Chicks with Chutzpah

A rOyal AdVentuRe

On July 15, a week before the wedding, Andrew had his stag night at Aubrey House with the likes of Elton John and Sir David Frost. I desperately wanted to gate-crash, but the fortress was impregnable: high wall, single entrance, guards with major biceps—no go.

As a fallback, Diana and I staged a hen night. With a few co-conspirators in tow, we donned gray wigs and dressed up in authentic policewoman outfits, down to our regulation dark stockings and lace-up shoes. After assembling just outside the Palace, we pretended to arrest one of our friends (chosen for her fabulous legs), who was playing the promiscuous lady.

The duty police at the gates thought this very strange. They called out the parks police, who proceeded to arrest the lot of us— even our protection officer, who played along—for causing a scene outside Buckingham Palace. They ushered us through some barriers and into their police van, and this was the worst part, because the other women slid slimly between the barriers, but I got wedged at the hip.

Diana and I had no intention of resisting. We thought it hysterically funny. We'd turned our engagement rings wrong side around, and it had worked, they hadn't recognized us.

After the van drove off and we sat down like little convicts, Diana asked the driver what kind of crisps he had on board and would he share them, please? Soon she was chomping away at these smoky bacon-flavored crisps. By the time we reached the end of the Mall, our cover must have worn thin—we heard one of the policemen say, "Oh my heavens, it's the Princess of Wales in drag!"

We got the van to drop us off near Anabel's, the big nightclub in Berkeley Square. And the people at the door said, "Sorry, we don't allow policewomen in here, it is a place for everyone to enjoy themselves." We coaxed our way in and pushed on to the bar—where whom did we find on their working night out but some eagle-eyed executives with the *Daily Mail*. We stood there shoulder to shoulder with them—ordered a round of orange juice, drank it down—and still they didn't cotton on.

Going out, we stopped traffic in Berkeley Square—we were having a wild time now—and headed back to the Palace near two o'clock in the morning. Knowing that Andrew was due home from his own little revelry, we told the duty police to get out of the way—and then we closed the gates. As it turned out, Andrew had just phoned from his car in advance of his arrival. When he saw the shut gates, he properly took it as something was very wrong. He flicked on his car locks, rammed the Jaguar into reverse, and screeched out around the Wedding Cake. He thought he was being set up.

It was about then that I wondered if we had gone a bit too far.

The morning after found me at breakfast with Mrs. Runcie, the wife of the Archbishop of Canterbury, who was to marry us. I could hardly see straight; I just barely made it through. (I do adore the Runcies; they've both been of such great support to me.)

Later I confessed our hen night to the Queen, and she thought it was reasonably amusing. We had got away with it clean—I'd been as naughty as I could be, and still I was adored by all. They were playing flush into my complex. I was wonderfully, extravagantly, madly brilliant. I could shoot a stag and hook a trout, and dance to *Swan Lake* in my wellies for good measure. I could do no wrong.

—SARAH FERGUSON, THE DUCHESS OF YORK

Fergie and Di giggling shamelessly.

The Bo*bb*y Sock Be*lle*s

We thought we were the cool crowd. Let's face it, we were. It was a Thursday night after our so-called sorority meeting of the Fidelity Sisterhood, where we met to pledge our undying love to God, country, each other, and never to wear white shoes after August. Our uniform: angora sweaters (chilly, since we'd been taught to store them tissue-wrapped in the freezer), little scarves knotted at the neck, and suede loafers or saddle shoes with bobby socks. We felt like the chosen few, and quite literally were, since the all-powerful Big Sisters determined membership by voting you in or, God forbid, out. In addition to member selection, the Big Sisters were sworn to teach us ladies' etiquette and life's finer points, such as the distinction between summer and winter jewelry and that the best way to get a guy was to play hard to get and wear pearls.

After the meeting, as if to release energy, we cruised. Sarah Jo's pale yellow '58 Buick was packed with ponytails, pink sweaters, and wild anticipation. We sat six abreast in the back seat, with room to spare. As we rolled past the entrance of a Victorian building all lit up, we knew by the stickers on the cars out front that we had come upon a gold mine. They were the convertibles of the U.S. naval cadets who were attending a dance. Quick assessment told us this was nirvana, because, after all, we were the chosen ones, and the girls inside were just girls. A battle plan was formed.

Since these were bona fide men of twenty-three and twenty-four, and not to be approached by the inexperienced, Peggy and I became

The angora-clad Fidelity Sisterhood.

self-appointed delegates to enter the dance and ask for help. Our credentials were impeccable—we had both dated midshipmen and flight instructors at the naval base, and we knew the difference between A-4s, T-28s, and T-33s (various aircraft, for the uninitiated). We elected two others to bend down over our car's dirty tires and let the air out. It worked! We scored big time with Paul Newman and Robert Redford look-alikes (recall the movie *An Officer and a Gentleman,* and you get the picture) who came out to rescue us ladies in distress.

I started seeing the Paul look-alike, and Peggy dated his friend, which made for great double-dating as we shared the secret of our caper between us, with the guys never suspecting. Two years later, I was invited to meet Paul's family, who lived in what looked for all the world like the plantation Tara, making me Scarlett O'Hara . . . or so I thought. There I learned that shorts were not acceptable attire at certain times of day and that Southern mansion dwellers have buzzers in the floor to step on when the servant is to bring in the next course of salty ham. It was during one of those elegant dinners that my juvenile behavior blew up in my face as I regaled my audience with the details of how I met Paul. In the silent aftermath of my tale, I sat uncomfortably with the realization that they did not find our trickery amusing. My Scarlett aspirations were completely checked shortly thereafter, when he became engaged to the admiral's daughter.

—RAE RUTH RHODES-ECKLUND

"Every time I think I know my friends,
they surprise me.
They are full of secrets I will never know."

—Vivi Abbott Walker, in
The Divine Secrets of the Ya-Ya Sisterhood, by Rebecca Wells

Alegra aNd I

Alegra and I were freshman roommates at University of California, Santa Cruz, better known at that time as Uncle Charlie's Summer Camp. Studying was almost unheard of when there was coffee to drink, music to crank, and gossip to share. The two of us were as different as we were the same; she had grown up among the Northern California redwoods, and I had fled the thick air of Los Angeles as fast as I could when I found out places like Santa Cruz existed.

Like soul sisters, we filled our days with easy conversation and comfortable silences. Some people said we looked alike, an observation I took as a high compliment since Alegra was many things I only hoped to be, and beautiful was one of them.

Today, like any other Saturday afternoon, we had our books spread in front of us in our tiny shared room with a view of the trees, made misty and damp by the recent storms. Alegra sat with her back to her bed; I was curled up on my bed, reading the same sentence about "basic" genetics three or four times. Halfway down my seventh page (7 of the 157 I was supposed to finish), I sighed and dropped my head to the pillow. From the way Alegra was softly singing the words to "Sugar Magnolia," I could tell she wasn't absorbing much either. It had been raining for days, weeks, and we were halfway to stir-crazy.

I closed my book and watched Alegra. She caught me, laughed quietly, marked her page.

"All I want to do is go outside," she said mournfully.

"I know. I just can't concentrate."

"We should just go out into the field now, even though it's raining," she said, alluding to the large grassy field at the bottom of the hill where we lived. It was less than a quarter-mile away, but it felt like acres of land stood between us and our usual sun spot.

"Yeah, whatever, girl," I replied. "You go get soaked. What I don't need on top of everything is to be sick right now."

"You won't get sick. Let's go. Now. Let's run." I could tell she was serious. I started to consider it. I was reaching for my

the full molly

Merry old England found itself atitter when the eleven members of the Rylstone chapter of the Alternative Women's Institute, a very proper women's service organization, created a calendar. Surprised folks opened the publication, and in place of the usual sunsets and pastoral scenes, they found the women of the club, aged 45 to 66, wearing strands of pearls—and nothing else.

"We partly did it out of devilment," said Miss July, Lynda Logan. Devilment paired with ample red wine, and the spirited comaraderie of the group, fortified the women's resolve to disrobe and pose for the photo shoot. Giggling madly as they attempted strategic coverage with plants and props, the shoot was "tremendous fun," according to Miss May, Moyra Livesey. The calendar raised over half a million dollars for leukemia research and was lovingly dedicated to Angela Baker's (Miss February) husband, John, who had died of the disease.

These cheerful, confident middle-aged women became an international sensation and inspiration for people everywhere who were tired of looking at what one Englishman called, "stick insects with pouty lips and pipe cleaners for legs." "The Calendar Girls," received thousands of letters from women saying that their bold spirit had restored their own flagging self-esteem. "We're in our 50s and it doesn't bother us," claims Miss October, Tricia Stewart, "and that seemed to come across."

shoes when she said, "Naked."

"What?" I snorted. "You smoking something and not sharing again? Like, I'm going to strip down in front of all these maniacs and just **streak down to the field.**" This was not something you did in L.A.

"Well, then you stay here. I'll tell you how it was." She started untying her hiking boots. By the second sock, I was over my consternation. I mean, who was really around? And anyway, who would care? The truth was, clothing seemed optional around here anyway, with people sunbathing nude all over the place on hot days. Why not rain bathing?

We stepped outside onto our tiny porch, bare feet recoiling from the cold cement, towels wrapped around us, barely. Alegra touched my hand. "On the count of three, we run. If we run fast enough, no one will even know what went by. One, two, three. . . ." We shot off the porch, heading down the familiar path, past our friends' doorways, past the offices, past the coffeehouse. No one was outside, and if anyone was watching us from the windows, we were moving too fast to know. The rain was pelting us, and our desperate attempts to keep the towels around at least our bottoms were quickly surrendered. At last, we felt the loamy forest floor under our feet, but we didn't stop running. It felt too good. Like we had leapt off the highest cliff and discovered we could fly.

I dropped my towel in a patch of high grass and ran alone until my legs gave out from under me. I found myself surrounded by bending field grass. I lay back, listening to my heart and breath, quick from the running and the daring. I could hear Alegra panting nearby. For one moment, everything made sense. We were pure, perfect. I stretched, and there was Alegra's hand, a spark of sisterhood's promise passing between our fingers.

We wrapped our drenched towels around us for the walk up the hill, not caring about how odd we must look. By the time we reached our door, we had come to a few silent conclusions: That our bodies were to be cherished, that some moments are meant to be seized, and that there is no feeling in the world like rain on an unashamed heart.

—JENNIFER BERNSTEIN-LEWIS

"Each friend represents a world in us,

a world possibly not born

until they arrive..."

—Anaïs Nin

the 5 friends every chick needs

When we were mere chicks, we always had a best friend. There were other friends, of course, but the word *best* was reserved for that one special sisterfriend, soulmate, forever buddy—no matter the situation, we only needed *her*. Like Miss America, there could only be one girl wearing that satin sash glittered with the words, *Best Friend*. While your childhood best buddy will always be the sister of your heart, geography, jobs, and life in general make that singular reliance on one another impossible. Part of growing up is expanding your heart and your circle of friends along with it. Like any good team, a girlfriend gang evolves because each woman brings a unique perspective or strength to the franchise. In that spirit, we think there are 5 chicks that every woman needs in her court. You can get by with fewer if they can multi-task.

the "I've Seen You with Braces and Bell-Bottoms" friend

This is the one that knows where you live. Not only literally, but that figurative place where it all began. You bonded over jumping rope, passing notes, and gushing over teen idols. She knows your family, how you crashed your first car into a pole the day after your sixteenth birthday, and she didn't laugh when you wore a 32 AAA bra. Your friendship is based on the deep roots that come from knowing each other through all the big and little events that propel us into adulthood. She understands where you are coming from and helps you get where you want to go.

the biological buddy

This is the friend that mirrors your family status. If you have children, so does she, and hopefully her kids are close enough in age to yours that you can bemoan the dilemmas of potty training or car seats together. You listen patiently to her stories about junior, nod in the right places and then it's your turn. You swoop in in a crunch to babysit or pick the kids up from school and vice versa. It's a beautiful thing. On the flipside, this friend may be the one among your group that, like you, doesn't have children. Together you celebrate your freewheeling status at fancy restaurants where you couldn't find a high chair to save your life. You go to museum openings, see movies with subtitles, and indulge in marathon shopping excursions. Don't call me before 9 AM? No worries about getting any guff, she too is still asleep.

your own personal Martha Stewart

She knows everything from how to get candle wax off your cat's ear to what color shoes to wear with a celadon silk suit. Need a recipe for champagne punch? She'll fax over five of them and would make the champagne if she needed to. Roof leaking? She's there with some shingles and tar that she happened to have in the workshop. She has every tool, every recipe, and every magazine article cross-referenced and indexed, and she's as resourceful as the FBI, CIA, and Interpol combined. She is irreplaceable.

your sister-in-a-suit

She knows how much your salary is and was instrumental in getting it there by counseling you before your last big performance review. You share investment tips, career strategies, and the secrets of crafting the world's perfect resume. What to wear to that interview? She's the one you turn to. Powerhouse, confidante, and the *Wall Street Journal* in comfortable pumps—she's a source of professional inspiration and awfully fun to have drinks with after work, to boot.

wild woman

You've always been curious about male strip clubs but never had the nerve to ask any of your usual friends to go to one. Bingo—wild woman is your ticket—she's probably done something crazy like work in one in the past. Nothing will shock her, and the word judgment (for better or worse) is not in her vocabulary. You can tell her anything. No matter how serious or benign, she takes it in stride on her way to the next adventure. When you're with her, hang on tight and never use your real name.

a Little *ni*GhT Mischie*f*

This isn't only my story. It belongs to all 258 of us who, in the fall of 1955, arrived at Saint Mary's College, a small women's liberal arts school in Indiana, with pie-in-the-sky dreams and pockets full of good intentions. Settling into the freshman hall, we unpacked our quilted poodle skirts, arranged our mandatory dresser scarves, and, as suggested in our freshman handbook, decorated our rooms with something "green and growing."

In spite of rigid rules and stiff curfews, we generally managed to stay in the good graces of our dean for most of the year—until an epidemic of spring fever, complicated by a severe case of exam jitters, struck unexpectedly in late May. As dogwood blossoms enticed our collective noses from our books, Dante, Dickens, and diameters gave way to seductive visions of dunes and warm sand between our toes. While we watched with envy from behind dog-eared Western Civ notes, indulgently carefree seniors, finished with exams and newly graduated, cavorted around campus in flagrant disregard for our sorry lot.

It may have started with the food fight that erupted among several freshman tables back in a corner of the dining room—an unheard-of occurrence, rendered possible only by the departure of the seniors, whose job it was to instruct the younger students on table etiquette and the art of conversation. Our laughter, sucked in and squelched between fork-flicked mashed potatoes, had never felt so good. The exhilaration of that tiny, insignificant act of anarchy galvanized us as a class. As we giggled and guffawed our way back to our hall, the plot thickened.

There's no question the troops were **restless and ready for a little harmless insurrection.** There was no instigator or mastermind. It was mob rule, plain and simple. Before long, a plan was formulated. We would strike late, after our ever-vigilant dean had gone to bed.

Focused as we were on the mischief of the moment, exams were the furthest thing from our minds. Between fits of giggles, my three roommates and I put on our PJs, brushed our teeth, smeared our faces with Noxema, and hurried to bed as soon as it was "lights out." We heard the dean make rounds. Then all was silent. Daring to communicate only occasionally with faint whispers or hand movements, we lay in bed waiting. Then, around midnight, we heard it! The horrific crash of a transom, about two floors above us, followed by another and another and another—like a volley of cannon fire. The noise—magnified four times over by cavernous linoleum halls, vaulted ceilings, and broad wooden stairwells—echoed throughout the building, from its bowels to its towers, like the deep belches of thunder on a summer night.

When the banging and the crashing started, I lay momentarily paralyzed, not expecting the sound to be so deafening. But as soon as the room next to us fired off their salvo, my roommates and I jumped into action. I'll admit I expected the dean to arrive any second, and prayed my father would understand my suspension, or worse, dismissal, while I watched Mary, Susy, and Connie take their turns lustily lowering and slamming the transom. When it was my turn, I

The troublemakers of St. Mary's College.

sailed out of bed, apprehension changing to exhilaration in mid-stride, and pulled the bar as hard as I could. As the resounding explosion catapulted down the hall to signal the next room, the four of us collapsed in a tangle of hysterical laughter.

Our hall nearly came off its foundation that night as we hit the transoms in lieu of books. With no way to signal an end to the clamor, bedlam continued well into the night. Hall monitors, class officers, and the dean raced around, not sure what to do or who to blame. They tried in vain to calm the foreign-speaking students who had not been taken into our confidence, as well as the elderly retired sisters who lived in the convent behind us. The police were called, and I think even a couple of fire trucks showed up. While we watched from our window, they were quickly dispatched, but their presence was enough to restore calm. After a couple more errant salvos and snickers smothered in pillows, silence reigned.

In the fervor of the moment, the consequences of our actions had never been considered, but we were not surprised to be called collectively on the carpet the next morning by the president of the college. Mass expulsion was a foregone conclusion.

After a short preamble, Sister Madeleva, a small birdlike woman, her face framed by a starched white bonnet atop a sea of black, walked among us and said, "Last weekend we had a graduation, and Miss Clifford was our valedictorian." She paused, looked at several of us, eyeball to eyeball, then asked, "Who was yours?"

I'd love to say that first one freshman, then another, and yet another stood, until the entire freshman class stood en masse to take full blame for what would infamously become known as the "Twenty-one Gun Salute." But, that only happens in the movies. Instead, the room grew deadly quiet and we all just sat there avoiding eye contact, our bravado reduced to a trickle, and waited. I'm sure I speak for us all when I say we were terribly surprised when one of our classmates, Pucky (Aurelia for short) stood to say she was. A low quizzical murmur went through the room. It was news to all of us. Only later would we learn that Pucky wasn't returning the following year and had therefore elected to be our sacrificial valedictorian.

To this day, I don't believe the president bought that bogus confession. I rather think she found it a refreshing interlude to a week of stuffy pomp and circumstance. She let Pucky have her moment of glory, then promptly campused all of us for the remainder of the term, hardly a punishment since, with exams, we weren't going anywhere anyway. The campus returned to normal, our parents were never informed of our prank, and we dutifully stayed in our rooms and studied. That is—until the doorknob incident.

But that's another story.

—Barbara Benford Trafficanda

Your rOOmMate's a Hawg

A friend of a friend of a coworker was looking for roommates. I was new to California, struggling my way through college, working full-time, and to put it mildly, money was tight. So I answered the call. Little did I dream that I was meeting surrogate big sisters and friends for life—Marie, Claudia, and Nancy. The day we moved in together was my nineteenth birthday. Amid the chaos and boxes, they insisted on a barbecue—Nancy even made me brownies with candles. I was blown away and have loved them like family ever since.

Claudia also brought a fifth roommate into our home—a horrible rude creature we named "the Hawg." Claudia had worked at a temp agency back home in Illinois and toiled in a number of thankless jobs, one of which was at a manufacturing plant where long, sausage-shaped bags called "hawgs" were used to absorb oil from the machines. She had deftly formed one, in balloon animal fashion, into a very striking semblance of the male anatomy and had given it to a friend at the plant. When she moved in with us, the friend promptly boxed it up and sent it as a housewarming gift, where, as the Hawg, it found a thriving career on the west coast.

The Hawg had a knack for showing up in the most inappropriate places. Imagine snuggling up on the couch with a date and finding a penis-shaped beanbag stuffed under the cushions of the couch. Or how about under your pillow, in the backseat of your car, in your laundry pile about to go to the cleaners, or proudly topping your pillow shams when your mom is visiting? The Hawg knew no mercy. Juvenile, yes. Silly, definitely. Hysterical—absolutely. We would go into fits of laughter with each appearance of the Hawg, and God help the witnesses who half-grinned nervously like we were all crazy.

After Claudia and Marie moved out to get married and Nancy relocated, the Hawg stayed with me, and I had the joy of introducing him to the next set of room-mates—Gina, Donna, and Jan. I knew I had two more soul mates when Donna and Gina howled at his first appearance—in Donna's bed. He also foretold the dark future for our relationship with Jan when she didn't find him the least bit amusing. She came storming out of her room, Hawg in hand, in the middle of Donna's dad's birth-day party demanding to know "What is this?" While we howled, Dad just shook his head.

chicks on the tube

When you are feeling a little overwhelmed by the testos-terone levels on the "boob" tube, remember that you can tune in to some great, past and present, TV gal pals:

Absolutely Fabulous

Any Day Now

Clueless

Designing Women

The Facts of Life

Friends

Girl Talk

Golden Girls

I Love Lucy

Laverne and Shirley

Oprah!

Roseanne

Sex and the City

Square Pegs

That Girl!

Two Fat Chicks

Two Hot Tamales

The View

We've all since **grown up** (sort of), made our own homes, and given the Hawg a rest. Nowadays he makes his appearances sporadically via the postal service on a special occasion or when we get together for group vacations or parties. He is so sly, so wily, that he always manages to keep his location secret. Just when we think he's retired, he pops up in the most embarrassing place. . . .

—AME MAHLER BEANLAND

"It seems to me that trying to live without friends is like milking a bear to get cream for your morning coffee. It is a whole lot of trouble, and then not worth much after you get it."

—Zora Neale Hurston

The Grady Hotel

Detrice and I have been friends longer than I can remember and sisters-in-law for more than half that time, since I married her husband Pete's brother, Buck. She is one of those magical people who has a way of attracting mischief and making you feel like the world spins a little faster when she's around. The stories I could tell. . . . But I'll share one of the tamer ones—don't want to embarrass anyone too badly.

It was the summer of 1959, and we were on our way to Sears and Roebuck in Atlanta for a big shopping trip—kids' clothes, curtains, and a little something for ourselves with anything left over. My niece Kay, who was twelve at the time, came with us. It was a long drive, and I remember how we were talking, listening to the radio, carrying on, and laughing—you can always count on laughing when Detrice is around. Detrice wheeled her station wagon into the lot and we headed into the store.

After an hour or so of shopping, Detrice nonchalantly said, "Bootsie, while we're here in the city, let's stop by the bar at the Grady Hotel and listen to some music." Just as coolly as if she did this kind of big-city thing every day. Since I'd never sat at the bar in the Grady Hotel in Atlanta and listened to music, I said that sounded fine, but what about Kay? "I'll fix her up," Detrice replied, leading her to the ladies' room. Detrice loves makeup and is a regular Michelangelo when it comes to application. She travels with every manner of brush, tint, and gloss in her purse, and she's not afraid to use it. In no time flat, she transformed Kay into a pint-sized thirty-year-old. A

Bootsie and Detrice on a recent adventure to see the
Sweet Potato Queens in Jackson, Mississippi.

stop by the makeup counter for a spritz of perfume, and we were clipping back out to the car.

Detrice drives like she puts on makeup—without fear. Careening into the parking lot of the Grady, she cut in front of an old man in a pickup and crunched into the parking space he was waiting for. In the process, she creased the entire left side of her wood-paneled station wagon along the bumper of a Cadillac. The old man was yelling at us, I was flustered, and Kay was beginning to cry. Detrice, calm as a deacon on Sunday, turned and said, "Now calm down, Sugar, you'll ruin your makeup. We'll tell Uncle Pete this happened in the parking lot while we were in Sears. Now come on. The band starts at eight." The old man, stunned at these two women and a little girl in heavy makeup, just shook his head.

I was a nervous wreck, but was so busy keeping up with Detrice's brisk pace I had little time to think of anything besides not tripping. Detrice put her arm around Kay and swept into the lounge with a passing wink to the bartender and a sugar-coated, "She's just real petite, Honey." Charmed, he grinned back and kept drying glasses. We tried to act sophisticated, but couldn't help but lapse into a few giggling fits as I sipped my greyhound, Detrice nursed a vodka tonic, and Kay stirred a cherry Coke.

All of a sudden, I became captivated by what seemed like an inordinate number of beautiful women sitting at the bar waiting for their husbands. They perched elegantly on their stools, hair perfectly coifed, with their hourglass figures brightly encased in daring fashions. Like exotic birds, they cooed and fussed over their mates as they joined them. My captivation turned to downright fascination when Detrice explained that they were not married to the men and that the warm reception was paid for. I'd never seen anything like that before. We took in the atmosphere, tapped our feet to the live music, and for a few hours tried our best to pretend like we were from Atlanta. Soon we'd spent all our money, but Detrice insisted on staying until midnight, when they served complimentary popcorn and treated all the ladies to a free drink.

At 12:15, after a stop in the ladies' room to wash Kay's face, we could hardly walk for giggling as we headed back to the bruised station wagon and cruised home, laughing until our sides ached. Pete was in bed when we arrived home, so Detrice had all night to mentally formulate her Academy Award-caliber performance of how the car was dented in the parking lot after we came out of the store—which was really the truth, minus a few details.

—Mary "Bootsie" Mahler

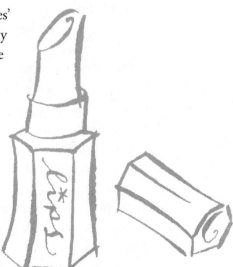

a Hair-RAising AdveNture

Let's just say I told Jody she didn't need a hair dryer in Africa, but she insisted. It was 1990, and Jody and I had just graduated from college, where we had been roommates for two of those formative years. We met on a hiking trip before freshman year and later bonded over cigarettes, boys, our mothers, and the answering machine. Jody was learning to play the guitar, and the only song she could really play was "Angie," by the Rolling Stones. In an effort to expand her repertoire, we spent hours trying to record our rendition of James Taylor's "Fire and Rain" on our outgoing message. Life was sweet. After graduation, in the ongoing effort to delay reality, we decided to spend some time abroad. She went to Nairobi to build housing for poor families, and I went to Israel to kiss foreign boys.

Many huts and hotties later, we agreed to meet in the Frankfurt airport to backpack through newly opened Eastern Europe. How we found each other among the teeming throngs I'll never know; it must have been the hair dryer-shaped bulge protruding from Jody's pack that innately drew me to her. In an effort to stay light, Jody would rip out the pages of *Moby Dick* once she read them, but God forbid she should part with her 2,000-watt dryer. Despite Jody's moveable hair salon (lest we need to be glamorous at a moment's notice), we were actually on a budget. So we hitchhiked east, to Prague.

Our first ride was with Gerald, a terminator-glasses-wearing German truck driver who spoke no English. Our next ride was with two American soldiers driving a red sports car. Although travel-weary, grungy, and decidedly uncoifed, we agreed to go with them to a disco. We fell asleep in their car and awoke the next morning, only to be dropped off on some rural highway median. We must have looked quite a wreck with particularly bad hair, because two German nuns took pity on us only minutes later. (At least they wear habits to compensate for bad hair days.) They drove us to the Czech border, and although I highly doubt we looked malnourished, they even gave us some yogurt and bread for breakfast.

The perfectly coifed pair in Prague.

We thanked them, got out, and walked the few hundred yards to the border. I must have had more of a spring in my step, or maybe it was just that my backpack was lighter without the hair dryer, but walking ahead, I noticed two cute guys in line standing near their car. We started chatting and learned they were officers in the U.S. Army. (We love the military.) Maybe it was luck, maybe they too were feeling charitable, or maybe they had been in Europe so long that they figured that even an American girl suffering from a bad hair day shaves her armpits. Whatever it was, we got to Prague, cleaned ourselves up, and had an unforgettable romantic weekend with the majors.

Now, almost exactly ten years and many hairstyles later, Jody has a new hair dryer, a husband, and a baby boy named Max. And I have had the chance to kiss some real foreign boys. It must mean I am getting older (or have better luggage), but now when I travel, I bring a hair dryer and always think of my adventures with my dear sister-friend Jody.

—Jill Pollack

"If you see someone with a stunning haircut, grab her by the wrist and demand fiercely to know the name, address, and home phone number of her hairdresser. If she refuses to tell you, burst into tears."

—Cynthia Heimel

B B B

Seventeen years ago, it started as a long weekend getaway to Myrtle Beach in South Carolina—a bridge group of eight women in their early forties, leaving husbands and families for some rest and relaxation. This trip quickly grew to a full week and now numbers ten women, including those who moved away and would not miss it for the world. A rented five-bedroom house right on the ocean is our retreat.

It is a collection of "all chiefs and no Indians." The personalities and talents are diverse, but nothing is ever held back. If you want to say it, you say it, and we go on.

Our conversation topics have changed over the years, but certain ground rules were set and have remained constant. We do not discuss our husbands. For the week they are referred to only as "them." Another essential to our beach vacation is that our peace is not interrupted by a ringing telephone. No one calls us unless it is a dire emergency. For goodness sake, it's seven days—stuff can wait. Other traditions include drawing for our rooms when we arrive, piña coladas on the beach at 11:00 A.M., and pimento cheese and tomato sandwiches for lunch. Our big midweek feast is steamed crab legs and shrimp served picnic-style on a large dining table covered in newspapers. Absolutely the best!

This is a **no-holds-barred time for bonding.** We share stories, laugh, act terribly silly, and sometimes become very serious. There are long walks on the beach, sunbathing, reading, and just

The BBBs sporting their signature T-shirts.

relaxing on the porch in a big rocker. We play all types of music. In the evenings, we turn it up loud and shag to that fabulous Motown music.

One summer, I arrived by airplane a day later than the rest. They had taken all my stuff with them, and agreed to meet me at the airport. It was a typical hot humid August afternoon. Since I work for the airlines and was flying standby, I was very professionally dressed. I sat next to a very dapper-looking businessman and excitedly told him about my friends and all the fun we would have. He wanted to talk, and I kept him entertained during the whole flight with my chatter about our group and what a diverse, talented, and sophisticated group of friends I was joining. He got off the plane with me, curiously watching to see who would meet me.

This group of normally fashionably turned-out women were standing by the gate as I deplaned. What a shock! I felt my face turning red. Each one wore shorts and a fluorescent pink T-shirt with three words boldly emblazoned in glitter across their chests: Beach Bridge Bitches.

They were covered in oily suntan lotion, sporting outrageous sunglasses, and had necklaces fashioned from seaweed and other beach "treasures." I was given a "Hawaiian" welcome, complete with a seaweed lei ceremoniously placed around my neck.

The other passengers and bystanders were thoroughly entertained and giggled their way past our wild-looking "Ya-Ya" group. They got just a small taste of what the week held in store for us.

—PEG BURLEIGH

"I've had it up to my ass with sedate."

—Thelma in *Thelma and Louise*

Jezzie

Have you ever been infatuated with someone? Not just a crush, or an attraction, but the insatiable urge to do something, anything, to become the object of another person's desire? That's how it was with my Kung-Fu instructor Tony. I was seventeen, and he was twenty-two. He had his own car, his own apartment, and an understated masculinity that I found enticing. He was tall, and lean, and muscular, and of course he was a top-notch martial artist (this ranks an A+ in the macho department, especially when handled in a humble manner). We needn't delve into the depths of his columbine-blue eyes or the punch in his step when he walked. His crooked smile or dry sense of humor probably wouldn't be of interest to you either, but suffice it to say I really had a thing for him.

At the same time, **I had a freaky boy-crazy friend,** whom we can call Jezzie (short for Jezebel). Jezzie was my friend because she was everything I wasn't. She was blonde, and she was chesty. She always had boys hanging on her every word, and she was chesty. She wore black underwear, and a black French bra, and she was . . . oh well, you get the picture. Anyway, Jezzie always got the cutest boys, and I got . . . well, I got to wave at them as they drove off in their hot rods with Jezzie. Jezzie often set me up with boys, but I was naive and kind of old-fashioned. She called it prudish. The fear of God (and more importantly, Mom) had been drilled into my head long before the onset of puberty. Boys seemed to somehow sense this, and so, by the tender age of seventeen, I had only been kissed twice.

By the time Tony began to pay me any attention, I had already pegged him as my one and only True Love. It would be like a Fred Astaire movie. He would dance (make that monkey-roll) over to me, wink, and perform a flying drop kick to my wondering amazement. Then, he would lead me to his awaiting chariot (a '75 silver Nova with tinted windows), and we would drive off into the sunset. He would beg me to marry him, and, not wanting to disappoint him, I would agree. We would have all the worldly goods a black belt would grant us. We would throw keggers for our friends, and I would be the envy of every girl. Tony would pick wildflowers for

forever in blue
(nail polish, that is!)

Katie Hayes and Lizzie Anders were the best of friends—London hip-hoppers working at the start-up MTV offices in London. Craving more adventure, the pair decided to leave their jobs and embark on an around-the-world-holiday. They made the obligatory shopping excursions to purchase gear—including blue nail polish for their toes. Their plan was to travel through Africa to Asia and on to Australia and New Zealand. For the last leg of the trip they hoped to purchase a purple VW van and drive it across the U.S.

The first month of their trip was perfect—encounters with wonderful people and fascinating sites. However, on their flight from Ethiopia to Kenya, they found themselves in a terrifying situation. Their plane was hijacked, then crashed into the sea near the Comoro Islands. Miraculously, both women survived but Katie was more seriously injured, and the two were separated. In the makeshift hospital, Lizzie begged her caretakers to find her friend, but with the language barrier and post-crash chaos, no one was able to identify and locate Katie. Finally, just as they were both about to be shipped off to different cities, a French doctor came up to Lizzie saying, "Zee blue finger sisters, they must be kept together!" He had recognized Katie thanks to their matching blue toenails.

Four and a half months after the crash and rescue, Katie and Lizzie resumed their travels. There hasn't been a day when they haven't sported blue toenails.

me every day, bring me coffee in the mornings, and spend hours gazing at me as I went about my daily routine. When we grew old, we would die in each other's arms, neither of us able to sustain life without True Love.

Jezzie had always been a faithful friend. She and I got along famously—she was raucous, loud, and wild, and I went along with whatever she did, usually laughing while hiding my face. She would make sure I didn't drink so much that I got sick when we went to parties. She would face down any girls who thought I was easy prey. She even (with an oh-so-sweet manner) talked my mom into extending my curfew a few times. She took me to my first rock concert—and my second, and third. She taught me how to smoke, and she showed me how short to cut off my cut-offs. We were best friends. Nothing could come between us.

So, of course I told her about Tony, that he was the one. She looked at me like I was sick.

"How do you know?" she asked.

"Well, he's been flirting with me an awful lot, and last Friday, he kissed me." My face turned red just telling her about it.

"Kissed you?" she asked. "That's it?"

"Jezzie!" I said, my face flushing deeper. She laughed, tousled my hair, and announced, "I'll just have to check this guy out."

It was August, and the weekend of her birthday, when she came by the martial arts studio to pick me up after my evening class. I introduced her to Tony, and she immediately turned on that charismatic charm that seemed to draw men like sweat draws flies. She produced a bottle of wine that she'd talked someone into buying for her.

Tony located some clean coffee cups, and the three of us had a drink in celebration of her birthday. Then she had another, and so did Tony. I abstained, wanting desperately to avoid making a fool of myself in front of Tony. After they had two glasses each, Tony asked her if she wanted to see his new car. She gave me one of her I'm just toying with him smiles, and they went to the parking lot together. I poured myself another half a cup and sipped at it while I waited for them. After I'd finished the wine, I began to watch the clock. Fifteen minutes. Twenty minutes. Twenty-five minutes. I was worried about them, so I snuck around the side of the building. I could see the car. They were nowhere to be seen. I was really getting ticked off when I noticed that the Nova was rocking like a cradle. I could even hear the shock absorbers squeaking.

Damn it! I thought, Jezzie, what the hell are you doing? Concern raced through my mind close on the heels of fury. I was really worried that they were doing what I thought they were doing in there. I'd never experienced it, but two girls had left school that year because they had gotten pregnant. I didn't want that to happen to Jezzie. I agonized over what to do. Finally I decided to stop them before Jezzie got more than she was asking for.

Murmuring the foulest curse words I knew through gritted teeth, and with knotted fists, I started toward the car. As I got closer, I realized that even with the darkened windows, I could still see in. I edged the rest of the way to the car with my back turned, and a hand (very obviously, I hoped) clasped tightly over my eyes. I banged on the window. The first try didn't work, as I could still hear the shock absorbers. I tried again, and kept banging loudly until I heard the squeaking stop. Then came the sound of panic-stricken muffled voices from inside the car. By this point, whether from nerves or the ridiculousness of the situation, I'll never know, I had a huge grin on my face. Fighting an overwhelming urge to laugh, I lifted my hand from the window and waved my most friendly wave. Then, with my eyes still covered, I made my way back inside.

When they came in, both of their faces were scarlet. I couldn't seem to get rid of my smile. Tony said good night and abruptly departed. Jezzie grabbed her bottle of wine, her purse, and said, "Let's go party." I followed her to her car, and as she started the ignition, still smiling, I said, "Well?"

"Nope," she said as we pealed away from the curb.

"Nope, what?" I said, starting to show some irritation.

"Nope, he's not the one for you!" she half-laughed, half-shouted. Seeing that I wasn't laughing, she became serious, and apologized with as much humility as I had ever seen her possess. I tried to be mad, but I couldn't. He was just a guy. She was my best friend. When I told her why I had come to knock on the window, she gave me her most sincere smile, and a look that said I was both foolish and blessed. Then she tousled my hair, turned up the stereo, and floored the gas pedal in an obvious effort to speed us to our next escapade.

Tony dropped out of my mind almost instantly. I still saw him during classes, but couldn't for the life of me remember what I ever saw in him. Still, the fact that he never mentioned Jezzie's name again, along with the wistful look he sometimes gave me, convinced me of one thing. I was thankful for the fear of God, and (especially) Mom.

—Cilicia A. Yakhlef

tHe dAnce Class

O nce again, my friend Sally and I have released our inner-crackpot crones. (Although I should record Sally's objection to the word *crone*. Five years younger than me, she prefers to be known as a *cronette*.) Three weeks ago, she called with news of a Japanese modern dance troupe, Buto-Sha Tenkei, that was coming to Houston. She couldn't attend their performances, but the company's dance master would also conduct a master class.

"Wanna go?" she asked.

"A master class?" I demurred. "We're not dancers."

"Oh, come on," she said. "You talked me into joining your dance exercise class. Besides, the class is for theater majors too."

"Okay," I said, "sign us up." Too late it occurred to me that the closest we came to being drama majors was our mutual talent for hyperbole.

I first met Sally in a yoga class several years ago when, after mutual groaning as we stretched in cobra, up-dog, down-dog, and sun salutation, she introduced herself and asked if I hadn't been in a short story writing class the previous spring. I was pleased that she remembered me, and we made a coffee date to talk about writing. We found ourselves meeting weekly, and soon we added Hallie, who had also been in our writing classes. Sharing writing led to sharing lives and then to mutual adventures, beginning with an overnight dream quest and labyrinth experience in a downtown cathedral. (Eighty women in sleeping bags in the sanctuary!) Next came backpacking in the Sierra Nevadas on a women's mountain pilgrimage and vision quest—twice. I, a devotee of spas, carried a 40-pound pack, dug holes for latrines, drank water from a lake, and loved it. We had also once purified ourselves in a sweat lodge, crammed into a tiny sweltering dark teepee with sixteen other women, praying and singing "Amazing Grace" for hours. So why not a Japanese master dance class?

So now Sally and I waltz into the community center, confirm our enrollment, leave our shoes at the door, and enter a large gymnasium lined with mirrors and folding chairs. Oh goody, I think, we get to sit and watch a demonstration. But she heads confidently for the middle of the floor, where hordes of long-limbed young people as supple as snakes stretch their bodies into shapes I couldn't have duplicated in utero. Sally and I are the oldest students by a score of years. She at least looks like a dancer; I could model for *matryushka,* the Russian nesting dolls. She's also wearing black, definitely the color of the day, while I have on pastel floral Danskin leggings and matching oversized T-shirt.

I gravitate toward a corner in the back, right in front of the folding chairs, just as dozens of junior high kids pour into the gym, filling them. No time to worry about our proximity as we rise to honor the dance master, a frail man, black beret slipping down a bald head, cocooned in clothing. After brief introductions through an interpreter, we move into a warm-up, making figure eights, swaying our bodies like trees, stretching our faces, pretending to chew gum. Repressing giggles, I carefully imitate the solemn-faced dance master.

Then we are passengers on a bus bumping down a country road.

Our irregular rows hang on to imaginary straps, heads, shoulders, and knees bobbing as we pantomime our ride. Next we become seaweed on the ocean floor. I close my eyes as we drift along with the current, the better not to see myself in the mirrors or the snickering students watching us with bored faces, this clearly not the field trip they had envisioned.

Next we become passengers on a space shuttle, blasting off the Earth with explosions of energy, then space walking with giant deliberate steps—children playing Simon Says take three giant steps. The twentysomething man in front of me with bleached blond crewcut, displays multiple nipple rings under his loose tank top. My concentration wavers. What does it feel like to have those installed?

Now we are balloons filling with air. As I sail along, a photographer, vest bulging with film and lenses, kneels for shot after shot, covering the room, even lying down to get a coveted angle.

Sally blissfully dances on, eyes closed in a trance. She looks disappointed when we are told to sit for question-and-answer time, but I sink gratefully, if not gracefully, to the floor. Someone asks if the dance master knows the history of butoh. "Hai," he replies, "yes." His interlocutor ventures another question; could he tell us then? Briefly he explains that butoh developed as a spiritual response to Hiroshima and Nagasaki. I wonder if he considers watching me dance seaweed sufficient revenge. I wonder if I do.

A teacher risks another request; since her junior high students will be unable to attend a performance, will the master demonstrate a brief routine? (Apparently she doesn't consider our class performance an adequate representation of a dance form described by its devotees as physical, spiritual, and intensely moving.) "No," he says, "come tonight."

Dismissed, we find our shoes and straggle out as the photographer asks those whom he photographed to sign releases. Sally and I are not asked. I pick up a brochure from the table as we leave and read that the English translation of *Buto-Sha Tenkei* is "Chickens from the Sky." Crackpot crone and cronette, we two heavenly chickens leave laughing. Too Westernized to absorb a Japanese spiritual climate in one dose, we have not found nirvana.

On the other hand, we've lost nothing but a morning.

—SuzAnne Cole

"Women get more radical with age."

—Gloria Steinem

The pearL Defense

Back in the '70s, I attended a two-year women's college that stood nestled in the foothills of the Catskills. It was here that I first met Barbara, on the first day of the first year of college. We were roommates, not by choice but by the draw of a lottery. I didn't like her at first; she seemed like a goody-goody, with her buttoned-up cashmere sweater and straight skirt. Besides, she was just a little "too thin" and I was secretly envious. But as time went on, we became fast friends. Barbara fell in love with a cadet from West Point and ventured there almost every weekend to be with him. Back at school, we all waited anxiously on the huge staircase for her to return with tales of her latest adventures and runs galore up her new Hanes stockings.

Once, I asked her to see if her boyfriend Earl could set me up with a blind date for the weekend. I was fascinated by the tales of West Point and all those guys in uniform, so she called Earl, and off we went in Barbara's VW bug. When we arrived, Earl met us, and I thought ten years had passed before they finally parted after a passionate kiss. I was ready to meet my man; I was excited and nervous. They were seniors, which meant that they could leave campus just as long as they were back in the barracks by midnight sharp.

We went to dinner. Barbara and Earl were inseparable, moving as one unit the whole evening. My date was a huge guy, a linebacker for the West Point football team. I liked him, but he was quiet—not the dashing, debonair date I had imagined all the way up in the car. After

XoXo

dinner, we found ourselves in Barbara's Volkswagen, driving along the Hudson River. It was a beautiful night with a full moon. Barbara had told me about a place called Inspiration Point, where everyone parked— very romantic, very exciting. I told her that if I was coming with her, she and Earl would have to restrain themselves for one weekend; Looking back, I should have known how impossible that was for them. As the car wound its way down the hill toward the water, I knew we had reached our destination. Barbara and Earl began their passionate embraces, oblivious to the world; the windows fogged up and the car began to rock back and forth. Before I knew it, *Wham!* There was my date, like a fallen building, right on top of me, sprawled across a miniscule backseat. He was all over me, and it felt like Seattle inside that car!

Now, if you are from the East Coast, you are most likely familiar with the "necklace trick." Everyone knew this one; if you were with a member of the opposite sex who was straying into bodily territory above the waist that he shouldn't be, just start fingering your pearl necklace. Both arms would block the desired area (in theory at least) and hopefully, you would get out of it gracefully.

That night, with this panting senior linebacker on top of me, we were way past the necklace trick. I had to think fast. So I blew my nose backward in a snort that was pretty impressive. It sounded remotely like one of those foghorns way out on the Hudson. "What the hell is the matter with you?" he managed to say. "Oh, didn't I tell you? I have this condition called postnasal drip." As disgust took its toll on him, he distanced himself as far over on the other side of the backseat from me as possible. Taking no chances, I continued to explain this malady to him in graphic detail. My friends in the front seat were oblivious, but eventually surfaced and we all drove back to West Point. I never saw that guy again.

Barbara and I laughed all night about it. She said we should patent my technique as a new form of protection against unwanted men. We have remained fast friends.

—Sondra Holtzman

"You've always been crazy.
This is just the first chance you've had
to express yourself."

—Louise in *Thelma and Louise*

shoo fly don't bother me

Ever set out for a fabulously fun night with the gals, only to have it spoiled by the arrival of some lecherous hangers-on of the male persuasion? Some of our chick friends have come up with creative ways of getting those overly persistent guys out of your hair (for the night, at least). Remember, these are powerful secret weapons only to be employed when all the standard, i.e., nicer, practices have been exhausted:

the man begone

Frantically wave your hands in the air and act like you are spraying an aerosol can. When the men ask you what you are doing tell them that you are using your "Man Begone" spray—tonight's party is strictly a chick thing. Wink and assure them it's no worse than mace.

the crying game

If you notice a shark circling your group, quickly grab a bar napkin and start "sobbing." We're talking loud, gut-wrenching sobs while your girlfriends pet and coo, "There, there." Girlfriends should join in on the wailing, grabbing more and more bar napkins for the inevitable loud nose blowing. Don't worry if the "sobbing" develops into hysterical laughter; it'll still sound legit.

the chick conference call

This requires two mobile phones or a pay phone close by. Have one girl-friend go off to the ladies' room and call one of you on her mobile phone or from the pay phone. When the phone rings, answer it and scream, "Ohmigod it's_____ (insert name of long lost sisterfriend)!" Quickly gather around the phone talking excitedly. Every time the lecherous one talks to someone in your group scream, "Ohmigod, she's right here!" and immediately pass her the phone.

the one-up(wo)manship

When the unwelcome one tries to impress you with his manly accomplishments, insist on talking about your feats. No matter what he's done, you've done it first, more often, better, and with superior style. And so has your best girlfriend. Drag her into the conversation so that she can add lines like, "Oh, you've only done the climb once—what's wrong? Ya got scared?" (Make chicken sounds.) "Well goodness! Did you *crawl* over the finish line or what?" (Make dog pants.) "Oh, scuba diving *there* is for wimps—you afraid of sharks or somethun'?" (Hum the theme from Jaws.)

"There are people whom one loves
immediately and forever.
Even to know they are alive in the world
with one is quite enough."

—Nancy Spain

2

Cherished chicks

Mad tea parTies

Ever since I was a little girl who wanted to be Alice in Wonderland, my idea of a good time has been a "mad tea party." And I am not alone. Like everyone else, my girlfriends and I are desperate for time. Between work, my boyfriends, and my own creative projects, my relationships with my girlfriends were getting short shrift, which makes no sense at all since that's where I get my nurturing. So I "date" my girlfriends. We give each other the special treatment: pick a fancy (mostly a low-budget glam) place to meet, get all dressed up, and go!

There is, however, a method to our madness. We go for tea. Let me tell you, this is one of the all-time-great ways to go around the world for the price of hot water and a tea bag. It seems that every culture has a different style and ritual for tea. The classic Western world's version is, of course, at three o'clock sharp in the afternoon, British high-style with the fanciest silver tea set available, porcelain cups and saucers, and scones, crumpets, jams, jellies, and cream. Maria, Leslie, Nancy, and I love to go for high tea in fancy hotels downtown.

After a fierce spate of shopping, we go piling in to the Saint Francis or the Mark Hopkins with our bundles and bags, dressed to the nines and sip away, pinkies curved just so. There is never a crowd, the service is impeccable, and we feel about as special as is humanly possible. You simply can't knock it until you've tried it. Making tea for the girls is pretty good, too, but it is difficult to match the service of a dapper old-school waiter who knows that taking tea is a magical experience.

Our thirst for tea now knows no bounds. We go to Japantown, take off our shoes, and squat down on Zen mats for green tea. We go Vietnamese for monkey-picked tea; we go Indian for steamy, fragrant chai; we go "hippie" for herbal organic; we go Middle Eastern for strong, sticky sweet Moroccan tea; and we go Chinese for blackest oolong. Didn't we feel special when all those reports about how healthy green tea is came out? We were way ahead of the pack on that one.

But it's not about the tea. Taking tea is one of the oldest "chick things," a time all to ourselves for sharing, laughing till we cry, telling secrets, and bonding as only a group of girlfriends can over a "cuppa tea."

—Brenda Knight

dynamic duo

You never know what might happen when the gals get together for tea . . .

On July 9, 1848, Elizabeth Cady Stanton and four other women gathered in a parlor in Waterloo, New York, for tea and ginger cakes. They found their conversation turning to their frustration and unhappiness over their treatment as women and the fact that they were not allowed to vote. By the time the last drops of tea had been consumed, these five women had conceived the idea for the first women's rights convention, which took place only ten days later in Seneca Falls.

Almost three years later, activist Amelia Bloomer introduced Elizabeth Cady Stanton to Susan B. Anthony, forever linking a dynamic duo whose partnership formed the driving force behind the women's movement. Upon meeting Susan, Elizabeth is quoted as saying, "I liked her thoroughly and why I did not at once invite her home to come to tea I do not know." Their immediate friendship blossomed when shortly afterward she invited Susan to stay with her and together forge an alliance to promote women's rights.

The two women complemented each other perfectly. While Elizabeth ran her home and minded the office, Susan hit the road. She was the legs of the operation—traveling, giving speeches, organizing rallies. Elizabeth was the words—writing speeches, drafting resolutions, and scripting the words of a revolution. While Elizabeth wrote and pored through laws, "Aunt" Susan baby sat and did chores around the Stanton home. Susan wrote, "My soul is in the work but my hands are with my family." Elizabeth's and Susan's political alliance and personal friendship spanned more than fifty years and thousands of cups of tea.

Neither would live to see the culmination of their efforts, for the struggle took seventy-two years—it wasn't until 1920 that women were finally allowed to vote. Your tea party or friendship might not result in the empowerment of 51 percent of the population, but then again, look at all you could do!

"I forged the thunderbolts, she fired them."

—Elizabeth Cady Stanton

"Failure is impossible." —Susan B. Anthony

The OriginAls

We were five women, ranging from twenty-eight to forty-one, all sailing friends, all wives, ready to celebrate a birthday among us. It was Jeana's big day, and we all converged at a local restaurant—aptly named Shenanigans. That evening we realized that beyond the love we all shared for water and sailing, we all shared a need for more "girl time" in our lives. So, after much discussion, we christened our group "The Originals." That's how we began: The Originals, established April 8, 1993.

We meet once a month, alternating as hostess somewhere locally, to celebrate birthdays, anniversaries, holidays, and just-because days. We have a scrapbook of pictures, and we chronicle our history in a journal, where we record events, shared feelings, and keep our club covenant:

The Originals' Covenant

Keep all secrets.
Have as much fun as possible.
Plan two monthly activities.
No dieting on "nights out."
No men.

We quickly decided that each member could add two addenda. So we have these additions:

Addendum 1: Have cold beer in the fridge.
Addendum 2: Always be there for each other.
Addendum 3: Always hug when we leave.
Addendum 4: Be loyal.
Addendum 5: Always stay friends.
Addendum 6: Be supportive.

At our inception, we elected a treasurer, and each paid dues of $10, with the goal of taking a group trip. After three years, we amassed a fortune sizable enough to get us all to Las Vegas for St. Patrick's Day. We rented a car and spent the weekend piling in and out of it circus clown-style. We even had our very own Elvis to show us around the town. (One of our members has a brother who greatly resembles the young, handsome version of the King, and he is indeed an Elvis impersonator in Las Vegas.) One night, we dolled up in our finery to star-gaze at the MGM Grand before the Mike Tyson fight. We had a great time until security caught on and showed us out.

Together we crewed an all-women sailboat, earning us the nickname "Ladies of the Lake." At holiday time, we rented a limousine and cruised around, viewing the Christmas lights. We have found that July is the hardest month to gather everyone together, so we suspend our gatherings in lieu of family vacations for that month. We do our part to support local restaurants and we're not afraid to have a cocktail. Our favorite libation is a snakebite—equal parts tequila and peppermint schnapps, sipped from little mugs. It's not a drink for sissies.

"There are no original ideas.

Like any good girlfriend gang, we are always excited to increase our numbers, and so far we've grown by two. The original members convinced the rookies that our group had initiation rites. The first new member **danced on the foredeck of our sailboat** while a local barge carrying 200 passengers cruised by playing "Proud Mary." She got off easy when you consider that our second enlistee had to wear a specially decorated witch's hat (think bachelorette party gone really bad) out to a Japanese restaurant, where she sampled sushi for the first (and probably last) time.

Sometimes it's hard for us all to be in the same place at the same time, but we celebrate with all who can attend the monthly gatherings. To date, we have one member who has *never, ever* missed a get-together. The one who started it all with that birthday on April 8. Congratulations, Jeana. The original Original.

—SHERYL ANN LEE, AKA DUFF

There are only original people." —Barbara Grizzuti Harrison

a diVine *en*cOu*n*ter

M y friend Callie and I were struggling to keep our compo-
sure as we rifled through the trunks of our parked cars in
the hospital parking lot. Laughing and teetering on high
heels, we were attempting to remove our business suits and get into
our outfits. Callie pulled a nightgown over her head and took her suit
off under the gown. I was doing the same thing with the aid of a
bathrobe draped around me. Then the *pièce de résistance:* we took out
wings and haloes, fashioned from wire and tin foil, and helped each
other strap them on. Finally we replaced our precarious high heels
with sandals and bedroom scuffs. With a satisfied *thunk,* we closed
the trunks, inspected each other triumphantly, and proceeded on our
celestial mission.

You can imagine the reception our "angel" getups garnered as we
crossed the parking lot and headed to the hospital entrance. People
lowered their eyes, as they often do when they approach something
unexpected in the midst of the expected and are not sure of an appropriate or safe reaction. In all our makeshift glory, we entered the hospital lobby, where the receptionist looked up at us and laughed out
loud.

We crossed the lobby to the elevator, pushed the "Up" arrow, and
waited. I clutched at a slipping halo, and Callie remarked that the
faulty connection must indicate insufficient angelic virtue on the
part of its wearer. I reattached the halo and quipped back that
cherubs sporting frilly nighties need not throw stones.

The giggling continued as the elevator arrived and we began our climb to the top floor. We flashed angelic grins of satisfaction as a steady chorus of chimes marked our ascent.

Quite unexpectedly, the elevator stopped at an intermediate floor. The door opened to reveal a man and woman, who took one look at our angelic finery and froze in shock. As I pushed the "Door Open" button, I announced, "This is it! You're okay. You've made it!" They both broke into laughter, and the man shouted "Hallelujah!" We finally emerged at our destination with one crooked halo, but with our divine apparel otherwise intact. The nurse laughed as she led us down the hall.

Our divine journey led to the recovery room and bedside of the missing member of our trinity—our dear friend Pat, who was recovering from a mastectomy. The three of us were extremely close. It's one thing to make a friend because you meet at school or work or through a hobby or a club. It's somewhat different when you make a friend because you see her every week at a women's meeting of Alcoholics Anonymous. That's how I met Pat and Callie. Pat and I were in our early fifties, and Callie was in her mid-thirties. We were from different places and held very different jobs and together formed a veritable hodgepodge of life experience. What we had in common was alcoholism, wicked humor, and the will to survive.

Over the course of several years of meetings, we laughed and talked and whined and sobbed and growled and yelled and got through the situations of living that baffled us and bedeviled us and scared us and energized us and inspired us and frustrated us. We inhaled and exhaled and cursed and didn't drink and didn't use drugs and were present in each other's lives on Monday nights, over telephone lines and coffee and meals and comedies and tragedies—through the "stuff" that makes up living.

Callie and I had been frightened for Pat—first because of the possibility, and then the terrifying reality, of cancer. "We've got to support Pat," we mumbled repeatedly to each other. We did reasonable and traditional helpful things, yet we still felt dissatisfied. Several days before she was to enter the hospital, we talked again about our concern for Pat and almost simultaneously said, "Angels! We always give her angel things. What if we . . ."

Pat was a practicing Catholic deeply committed to her "HP" (Heavenly Person). She always wore an angel pin, and her home was filled with every form of angel she could acquire. Callie and I kidded her about being an angel junkie whose expanding collection would force her out on the street, but Pat knew that angels watched over her and those she prayed for. There was no better way to cheer and support her than in the guise of her most loved beings.

Pat's daughter and three-year-old granddaughter were there when we arrived. While we "hovered" over her bedside, fluttering our wings with a singular lack of angelic grace, hospital employees and ambulatory patients who had heard of the visitation came to join in the love and laughter in that room.

Some years have passed now, and the three of us still talk about the angel episode. Pat has been free of cancer since her mastectomy, and all of us have held fast to our sobriety. Pat reminds us that her granddaughter learned to see angels as a living reality that day and talks about her gratitude to us for our friendship and support. Callie chuckles about the parking lot and the people in the elevator and the outrageous joy for us in what we did. What I know is that my friend's response to a female terror and the presence of loving women in my life have enabled me to become the friend I always wanted to be.

—KATHERINE CLYMER

"Female friendships that work
are relationships in which women help
each other belong to themselves."

—Louise Bernikow

chick reads

Nothing bonds girlfriends like shared books, and no chickcentric library would be complete without these.

Little Women, by Louisa May Alcott. A classic tale of sisterfriendship.

The Heart of a Woman, by Maya Angelou. Soul food for a gal's spirit.

The Robber Bride, by Margaret Atwood. Nothing makes you circle the wagons like a wicked villainess.

Emma, by Jane Austen. A beloved busybody.

Girlfriends, by Carmen Renee Berry and Tamara Traeder. The name says it all.

The Sweet Potato Queens' Book of Love, by Jill Conner Browne. An action and attitude packed guide to life.

Sister of My Heart, by Chitra Banerjee Divakaruni. Friends are the family we choose for ourselves.

Fried Green Tomatoes at the Whistle Stop Cafe, by Fannie Flagg. How often have you wanted to "Towanda" something?

Practical Magic, by Alice Hoffman. You'll be charmed.

Patty Jane's House of Curl, by Lorna Landvik. Behold the power of the beauty salon.

Where the Heart Is, by Billie Lets. A good ol' girl triumph.

How to Make an American Quilt, by Whitney Otto. The power of crafting things together.

Wild Women, by Autumn Stephens. How the West was really won.

The Joy Luck Club, by Amy Tan. Generational soul-searching.

The Bad Girl's Guide to the Open Road, by Cameron Tuttle. Forget American Express, don't leave home without this book.

Divine Secrets of the Ya-Ya Sisterhood, by Rebecca Wells. A must for "girlfriend literacy."

Sheroes, by Varla Ventura. Let's add this word to the dictionary.

Goddess in the Kitchen, by Margie Lapanja. We love her motto—Eat dessert first. Start with the Magic Double Fudge Brownies on page 136.

Uppity Women of the Renaissance, by Vicki León. A rollicking herstory lesson.

Doorknobs *from* Denmark

In the past thirty years, Nancy Roberts and I have journeyed more than 50,000 miles together. At times our entourage included children, husbands, and beloved and not-so-beloved pets, such as Charlie, Jin Jin, Fluffy, and an ungrateful smuggled-in-my-pocket rodent who showed his gerbilly lack of appreciation by nipping me repeatedly during a transcontinental flight.

One rock of our relationship is Nancy's ability to build memories. Her mortar is tact, sensitivity, and the depth to recognize the defining moment in an otherwise commonplace situation. My grandmother loved Nancy for many of these same qualities. When my grandmother's stories—watching foxes play in the woods, and hiding from her mother in the top of a huge cherry tree until the scattered pits on the ground from the cherries she ate gave her away—began to stir a yearning within me to find her ancestral home, Nancy and I packed our bags.

Copenhagen, Denmark. July 1996, 2:00 A.M. in a hotel room near the airport:

"Do you smell something burning?"

"Yes, I think it's the ancestral doorknob!"

"How can a doorknob smell that bad?"

"Any ideas on how to get this thing through customs?"

Our search had begun the day before in the tiny town of Fodby Alt, Denmark, on the Fourth of July. At 9:00 P.M., it was still daylight, even though a steady rain flooded the streets. Nancy's steadfast commitment to my search gave me the courage to begin knocking on doors to ask if anyone knew the location of the Hansen family farm.

At the second house I approached, a lovely young woman took up my cause. She plunged into the gloomy rain, and as we splashed along, we began to pick up a small queue of supporters. Our group now numbered five sodden, cheerful Danes who appeared delighted to assist an American in her quest for her roots. It was late, and as the search went on, it was clear that continuing would mean missed hotel reservations, and that our promised relaxing day in Copenhagen would not happen.

My grandmother's home was in Old Fodby. We crossed the road and entered a lush forest glade, with a large fallen log lying in the road. (Did I see a quick streak of a red fox blur under the log?) Then a turn in the road. (Was that a huge cherry tree?)

There it stood, a large white square house built to last some 500 years ago. (Do the storks still nest on the chimney?) A young American couple had recently bought and remodeled it. However, a fire had obliterated all their hard work. A huge black hole in the roof covered with plastic sheeting was visible from the road, as was a dumpster filled with smoky castoffs. A young man appeared from inside the home.

"Could we see the interior of the house?" I inquired.

"Sorry, not today."

I looked at Nancy for help, and saw that she was distracted by the contents of the Dumpster. Nancy respects and cherishes fine old things and can find beautiful, useful items anywhere. Where I see junk, she sees heirlooms. She once pulled all the crystal knobs off the doors of a soon-to-be-demolished hotel and fitted them in her own home. Now her eyes were fixed on another doorknob. Lying beside the Dumpster was a charred door, and fused to the door by the heat of the fire was a wooden doorknob.

"Karen, you need a doorknob from your grandmother's house!"

We pulled, pried, and coaxed. The thick wooden door would not relinquish its prize. Finally, a hacksaw freed the knob, with a substantial piece of the door still attached. (Nana's voice in my head: "Oh, Carn, that beats all.")

As we drove away with this unusual memento, the picture of Nancy standing in the rain on a narrow farm road in Denmark was fixed in my memory. Who else could have found grace and closure to my search in a scorched slab of blistered wood and a doorknob?

Now, when I look through that perfect keyhole to my small piece of Nana's estate, my memories of my grandmother come into focus. I see her shaking her head in amused wonder that anyone would be so fortunate in life to have found a friend like Nancy Roberts.

The heirloom recovery specialists.

—KAREN MILES

OutruNning tHe Train

I t's a chilly day in February when I find myself walking in my old hometown neighborhood for the first time in almost twenty-five years. I had no intention of going this far when I left my parents' house to get a little fresh air.

I pull my jacket tighter around me as I study the shabby houses, amazed at how time has changed them. Memories and voices come back to me as I walk.

Softball games in the street: "Denise, throw it here! You're out, Diane!" Walks in the creek at the bottom of the ravine: "Ooh! Feel that squishy clay between your bare toes!" Kick the Can games in the alley: "All-ee-all-ee-in-come-free!"

My thoughts are interrupted by the lonesome call of a distant train whistle. I haven't noticed that sound in ages! Hearing it, I think of another train whistle, long ago, when Denise and I were about ten years old.

Denise became my best friend from the moment I moved into the house next door at age nine. We discovered over the picket fence that we were exactly the same age. Denise was the most fascinating person I had ever met. She had blonde hair, such a contrast to my own dark locks. Her eyes were a beautiful blue, the exact same color, she told me, as her September sapphire birthstone ring. She was vivacious and animated, whether she talked or played, yet patient and calm at the same time. She did have a temper, but it was slow to rise and quick to leave. An excellent athlete, she was competitive, but she always played fair. I can still hear her high-pitched giggle of a laugh and see that radiant smile. And what a flirt she was, batting those long straight eyelashes around, blushing beautifully at every opportunity. Inseparable through our grade school years, we were never indoors, if we could help it. We found a new adventure almost every day.

Another blast from the train whistle. I smile, thinking of Denise and me those many years ago. It was not unusual for us to walk, roller-skate, or bike all over town, but we did stay clear of the river. It was muddy, wide, cold, and usually filled with log booms. It was in a seedy area of town, too.

In those days, the bridge across the river was a single lane about a half-mile in length, shared by car traffic and the five or six trains a day that passed through town. One day, we decided to walk across, just to see what the other side was like. Surely we would hear the approaching whistle in plenty of time if a train came.

We were perhaps fifty yards across the bridge when we heard that train whistle blow. Panicking completely, we ran as hard as our legs would carry us. We could hear the train coming right behind us, blowing its whistle furiously.

Finally, we were on the other side, gasping for air. We had made it! We felt as though our pounding hearts would explode as we watched the train roar by. Then it dawned on both of us at the same time—why didn't we run the other way?

Thinking about that long-gone day, I sigh and continue walking. I am at the top of the hill now, looking down at the place we called "the Desert," which wasn't a desert at all, but a meadow. I gasp as I look down—it is completely gone, replaced by houses and apartment buildings. Our letters . . . what happened to our letters, I wonder. Did anyone find them, or were they just buried further by the heavy construction equipment?

The summer we turned twelve, Denise and I found a bundle of love letters in a deserted house down the block. They were written by a young couple at the time of World War II. We didn't know if the couple were married or not, but we could tell they were madly in love. The letters were in a neat little packet, tied together with a faded blue ribbon. They had been important to someone . . . and yet, they had been discarded and deserted. We were completely smitten with this romantic mystery.

Deciding our letters needed a proper place for safekeeping, we sealed them in an empty mayonnaise jar and buried them at the Desert. We vowed to come back for them someday when we were grown. We never dreamed that the Desert would be gone.

Tears run down my face. We never dreamed Denise would be gone, either. We never imagined that she would fall victim to breast cancer at age twenty-eight, leaving behind two daughters who were only four and six. That was fifteen years ago. Did Denise ever get the chance to tell them about the letters? Or the train? Or any of the other things that happened to us? Somehow, I doubt it. As I stand here, looking at what once had been our meadow, I vowed to find Denise's girls and share with them the memories of our special friendship.

—P. Diane Truswell

"She is a friend of my mind.
She gather me, man.
The pieces I am,
she gather them and give them back to me
in all the right order.
It's good, you know, when you got a
woman who is a friend of your mind."

—Toni Morrison, in *Beloved*

Zen *and* deStrucTio*n*

It always starts out fairly tame. "Yeah, just a nice, fun girls' night," we say on the phone. "We haven't see each other in a while. We badly need a fix of one another!" we all say. "*Yeah!* Okay, next Saturday it is, and we'll rent a hotel room so we can get extra crazy!"

It started when some of us who met in college were living in Spain together for four months when we were twenty years old. Experiencing the perils of disorganized travel, we learned what it was like getting lost and sleeping on park benches. Swatting flies away from each other's faces, while the other slept, little kids staring at us ("Are they homeless?" they would ask their parents.), kinks in our necks from resting our heads on our bulgy purses. Finally, managing to wake and find our hostel, still so tired from a restless and cold night. Dirty, cold, and exhausted, we bonded for life.

Now we all sit in the hotel room, playing the famed Chatty Cathy, Who's Next? game, telling each other the latest on the men in our lives, work, pondering what our missions in life really are (for the 354th time). . . . We're waiting for the last posse member to arrive; in the last outing, we initiated Alison, our newest passionate friend, into the group. For initiation, we made her walk down busy city streets, pulling her shirt up, flashing as many good-looking men as possible. "Good job, Al!" we all cheered. We were rolling in laughter.

At nineteen, Whitney and I had gone to Mervyn's to see if they had any cute hair accessories to wear to our bachelor-filled house parties (It seemed we were 24/7 on the hunt, so we had to look good!). We walked out with everything, except what we had walked in for. We did buy two pairs of red sequin baby slippers for our unborn baby girls, though. We thought, "Oh my gosh, would these be the cutest for Halloween; we could dress our girls as little Dorothys from The Wizard of Oz. Now, this was extremely funny, as Whitney and I did not even have serious boyfriends at the time, nor were we anywhere close to having children! To this day, six years later, we haven't lost the darling shoes, although they, along with us, are still waiting for our adorable long-time boyfriends to propose.

Being passionate dancing queens, we started the get-together this evening at La Bodega, a place that truly brings you back to your Spanish roots, even if you don't have any! While watching beautiful women dancing flamenco, we began by drinking wine out of the server's leather canteen. It made about twenty rounds before we gave it back. "Kathleen, drink more! You haven't caught up to the rest of us yet!" a couple of us ordered loudly.

There Michelle and I sat—in our apartment in Madrid, many, many miles away from home. I had gotten an urgent call that left me sobbing ice-cold tears. I had lost the second important man in my life, my sweet grandpa Joe, the gentle giant who had helped raise me after my biological father was kidnapped and killed. Michelle was consoling me, holding me, while I told her all the details: he had been found in the garage, with the car motor on. My little brother had witnessed paramedics trying to revive him. He was dead. Suicide. I felt so, so low, yet Michelle supported my broken heart and helped me continue my student life in Madrid. "Everything, even pain, happens for a reason," said Michelle. "Continuing life, learning from this experience will make you an even better person."

With warm, sangria-filled tummies, we stole someone's taxi. "If you snooze, you lose" is our motto. By now, we were cigarette-smokin', hyena-laughin' drunk ladies headed to Harry Denton's for some free drinks from our adorable bartender friend. After two shots, two lemon drops, one cable car, and a couple beers apiece, we were roarin' to get to our next and final destination: an underground club.

We had not had time for ourselves in quite a long time. So, over e-mail on a random Wednesday afternoon, Vicky and I decided that we would escape to Big Sur for a quiet, introspective writing weekend. Since high school, Vicky and I had always been the two in the group who passionately enjoyed journal writing, reading, and discussing what we had learned from our latest literary adventure. Throughout our two and one-half days at Big Sur, we did all sorts of wonderful "getting back to me" things. We gave each other writing lessons on what we had learned in our respective writing classes at UCLA and the Institute of Children's Literature. We hiked. We listened to audio books on memoir writing and creativity at work. We talked about our dream literary jobs, mine in Marbella, Spain, Vicky's in Provence. "Twenty years from now, even though we'll be really busy," we said, "we must keep doing these mini-escapes. They're chicken soup for our tired souls!"

Trashed. Absolutely trashed. We manage to get into the underground club without paying a cover charge. I promise the bouncer that if he lets us in for free, we will make sure that everyone around us has a great time. "Come on. Five beautiful women, we'll most certainly liven the place up!" And to that promise, we deliver. We're loving the

"Well darlin', look out.

music, singing out loud, dancing, and overall livin' *la vida loca!* "Life is so great!" we all keep repeating. As we always seem to do, we keep raising the bar for our dares. Instead of fairly easy requests like two of us walking over to a good-looking guy and freaking him, one of us shouts in the center of our dancing huddle, "Okay, you guys, let's take our shirts off!" Without a blink, one by one, we start taking our shirts off. Nervously, we look around, not because we are afraid of what people around us will think, but because we're afraid of getting kicked out (and, we knew what that was like because we had experienced it a couple times before!). So, there we are half-naked and loving it!

Back at the hotel, at around 4:00 A.M., we order pizza for breakfast. We talk and talk about our hot August night. We try to guess where a couple of us lost our shoes, why we have bruises all over, and how we got so drunk. Well, we knew, but it's always more fun to say, "Oh my gosh, how the hell did we get so drunk?" It makes for better storytelling to be able to relive the night's events all over again. And that's what it's all about—stories, memories.

And so, zen and destruction live on in us. Those deep "I understand you" moments as well as the wild and crazy moments we have with close friends that truly make you feel immortal. It's this web, the yin and yang of experiences that keep us sane, that aids us in enjoying life to the fullest. May zen and destruction live on in every one of us.

—MICHELLE GHILOTTI

My hair is coming down." —Thelma in *Thelma and Louise*

chick cheers

Most of us chicksters love to bond over drinks—be it sun tea, martinis, hot cocoa, or some other luscious libation. We have drinking rituals that we treasure together. Here are just a few ideas from girlfriend groups that you might want to try with your own gang.

pinkie-wagging high tea

Hosting a formal high tea sounds daunting, so don't do it. Opt for an interpretation of this British art form and invite your girlfriends over for an afternoon of girl talk and dainty sipping. Whether you go all out and polish up your tea service or just boil some water, the fun part here is to have an array of different teas to try, from exotic fruit-infused blends to simple herbal standbys. Make finger sandwiches and scones (or better yet, pick some up at a bakery). Play dress up and invite the girls to wear hats and pearls.

feeling hot-hot chocolate

Perfect for rainy days or cold winter evenings together—the homemade version is best.

quick chick hot chocolate (yields 1 serving)

1 cup of chocolate milk
4 tablespoons marshmallow crème
mini chocolate chips
fresh mint sprig

Combine chocolate milk and 3 tablespoons of marshmallow crème in a microwave-safe cup. Microwave until hot (2-3 minutes). Stir to dissolve crème and top with remaining tablespoon of crème. Sprinkle generously with chocolate chips and garnish with mint. (For extra warmth, add a small shot of Kahlua or Bailey's Irish Cream.)

saki it to me

Put some soft pillows on the floor or hit your favorite Japanese restaurant to enjoy this lovely Japanese offering with your buddies. Even more fun if you can get one of those private rooms at a restaurant and really pour the saki.

milkshake it up

Such little effort, such splendid results. Dump a couple of scoops of your favorite ice cream and a little milk in the blender. Toss in accompaniments like fresh berries or chocolate shavings. Pour the results into tall glasses with straws, top with cherries, and voila! You have a scrumptious offering for sweet fellowship.

fit for a queen margaritas

These tasty treats are one of the many libations of choice that Sweet Potato Queens imbibe when they are not waving in a parade in Jackson, Mississippi, or trying on trashy lingerie in a tour bus. They swear by a recipe that calls for limeade, Corona beer, 7-Up, and "really good tequila." If that sounds too wild for your taste buds, there's the other SPQ, endorsed margarita makings called Fat Mama's Knock You Naked Margarita Mix. You too can drink like a Queen by ordering the potion from The Everyday Gourmet (a Queen-owned and -operated establishment in Jackson, Mississippi), at 800-898-0122. Here's to your majorette boots!

"We love the name. We find that just saying the name makes us feel festive, which is, of course, a favorite Queenly feeling."

—Jill Conner Browne, on Fat Mama's Knock You Naked Margarita Mix

martini madness

Longing for a little glamour? Wrap your head in a scarf and lip up in bright red. Swank out your place with some appropriate tunes like *Wild, Cool & Swingin'* from the Ultra Lounge series by Capitol Records and call all your cool kittens over for a retro retreat. This is not your daddy's martini party…

the classic cosmopolitan

4 parts vodka
2 parts triple sec
2 parts cranberry juice
1 part fresh lime juice

Pour ingredients into a shaker with ice. Shake it all together, and strain into martini glasses. Garnish with a twisted sliver of lime or lemon peel.

Be*a*n h*o*llo*w* B*e*a*c*h d*a*y

Thirty-one years ago, when my friend Allison and I were little, we played together. We were the Lone Ranger and Tonto galloping through prickly weeds in the backyard. We were roller-skating champions, racing across the slickest stretch of pavement in the neighborhood. We were grown-ups promenading from my house to hers, she, a freckle-faced strawberry, in her mother's pink chiffon dress and I, an olive berry, smart, in white gloves and open-toed high heels made of green alligator leather. We did not know then that having breasts could be anything but gloriously grown-up.

One morning, seven years ago, I found out differently: Slippery and soapy in the shower, I felt a pebble-sized node. It was malignant. After the cyst biopsy and mammogram, I finally found myself facing the surgery resident. "How are you feeling today? Your pathology report shows malignant breast cancer," she said clinically. For the next few months, I alternated between shock and outrage. I was sure of one thing, though. I refused to lose my breast. Instead of a mastectomy, I chose a tylectomy, removal of the tumor and adjacent lymph nodes, and radiation. That combination has been a standard procedure in Europe for years, only recently gaining favor in the United States. After my surgery, I faced a regional tumor board and reluctantly agreed to adjunctive chemotherapy. No one, however, could offer a guarantee against recurrence.

And so, after my fifth infusion of chemo, I was particularly glad when Allison and I played again. On a shiny spring day we climbed into my little Honda Civic for a drive down the craggy California coast. The Pacific Ocean stretched westward, a glistening tabletop of aquatic motion. Bean Hollow, our favorite beach came into view; bright reflecting sand and cloud shadows called to us. Barefoot, we ran through the stinging surf. We ran, and ran, laughing. My eyes, light sensitive from the chemotherapy, blinked salt droplets. Soon, too much cold curled my toes. I rubbed them warm with a sun-baked towel.

Chemotherapy, I had been told, would zap any cells that had broken free from the original tumor site and had traveled elsewhere in my body. At least, my kind of cellular mutation, one of the "garden variety," was more responsive to treatment than some of the other known fifty types. Not all of the 175,000 women newly diagnosed each year in the United States are so lucky. I was beginning to appreciate the complexity of the disease, and my good fortune.

My spirits were high when Allison and I left the beach. When I turned south onto cliff-hanging Highway 1, known for its dangerous zig-zagging, Allison cautioned me, "You're driving too fast." She was right. I was going 40 miles per hour in a 25-miles-per-hour zone. For me, breaking limits was unusual, I am generally cautious, not wanting to be caught for any real or imagined infraction. But at that moment I was galloping high! Salt spray and dazzling light; gritty high—sand between my toes, underneath my fingernails. Sea-washed high! I was so glad to be alive!

As I lifted my foot off of the accelerator, I sing-songed to Allison, "I have cancer, what can they do to me?" Her eyes, growing into large hazel saucers, stared at me. I giggled. "Nothing! They can't do nothing." After a moment, Allison's crowsfeet crinkled and the golden highlights returned to her eyes. "I'm free," I whispered. Together we giggled and giggled.

That night, in front of the fire, as I thought about the 40,000 women who would die of breast cancer that year, I asked Allison, "Are you afraid of losing me?" A log hissed, spitting tongues of blue-white flames during the long moment before she answered, "I would miss you terribly." Another log split apart, "But you seem less frightened now facing death, than before, when you worried over everything. Knowing that you feel free makes my grief easier."

What Allison didn't know, couldn't know, (and neither could I) was that even today, years later, every single time that my physician orders a new set of diagnostic procedures, I panic. Every time the radiologist or the pathologist tells me, "It's negative," I cry. And then, outside the medical office, set free for another four months until the detectives must again investigate for cellular malfunction, I look for the Bean Hollow Beach Day with Allison, the cloud shadows, the green-blue swirls of textured motion; and again I feel my icy, sand-dusted feet rubbed with a towel warmed by the sun.

—Ilana Girard Singer

"A friend can tell you things you don't want to tell yourself." —Frances Ward Weller

a PlayHouse pArty

Whan JoAnn picked up the phone, I knew she could hear the weariness in my voice: "Jo . . . I need a Playhouse Party." Without hesitation, JoAnn replied, "You're on. Eight o'clock? I'll call the others." I was grateful for Jo's ability to take charge.

The others are an assemblage of about twelve women friends—no, not women friends, *girlfriends.* Not everyone would be able to come, but a core group would be there. Most of us had attended high school together, and within the group were a couple of sets of sisters like JoAnn and Linda, Jan and me. Together we comprised what we simply called "the Girls' Club"—a circle of friendship that began almost twenty years ago.

It was my older sister Jan who hosted the first Girls' Club event. At that time, some of us were still single, some just married, and a few had small children. We had drifted apart after school, but one day Jan invited us and our children to a pumpkin-carving potluck. We had such fun gathering around hot dogs, steaming bowls of chili, and apple cider, helping the kids carve their pumpkins, talking, laughing, and connecting again. We talked about how great it would be to meet regularly. Eventually the club evolved into monthly meetings, highlighted with seasonal events.

A Playhouse Party, however, is different. It is spontaneous, called with a sense of urgency when someone needs to talk. JoAnn and Larry live in a lush, midwestern suburb; their house boasts an expansive backyard where years ago Larry built a spacious playhouse for his two daughters. Complete with Victorian gables and shutters around the windows, it was a much-loved play spot for their girls when they were younger. Now it's where the Playhouse Parties take place. All the little girl stuff has been put aside except for the table in the middle, always freshly dressed with flowers from the garden, and plenty of pillows to lounge on.

Clearing the dinner dishes with my two not-so-willing teenaged children, I start to breathe a little easier knowing that soon I'd be surrounded by my girlfriends. It is a bit unusual that in the last ten years, many members of the Girls' Club have moved to the same west county suburb, 30 miles from our old haunts. It is fortunate, also: we are grateful for the close proximity.

Just before dashing out, I pulled a brush through my hair and saw myself smiling in the mirror, as I recalled the first time we met in the playhouse. It was an especially hot Fourth of July, as it only gets in the Mississippi Valley. *Stifling* was too kind a word. We were at JoAnn's pool party. Some of the guys were starting the barbecue, and the girls were lounging poolside, watching the kids splash around. We huddled around Linda, trying to get the latest scoop on her marital discord. But like radar, a kid or husband would call for one of us to watch a new trick, referee a disagreement, or find some barbecue tool. We tried moving to the kitchen, but had a trail of goslings behind us and a stream of guys coming in for beer. Finally, with a couple of dads on lifeguard duty and fresh margaritas in hand, JoAnn led us to the playhouse, and we ceremoniously shut the door. Linda was so ready to let it out, she yelled, "I'm not making another

The Playhouse aglow with candlelight.

dinner for that big jerk!" We roared, reveling in the freedom to finally speak openly.

Shortly afterward, one of the girls was in a serious family situation. We rallied around and called for an emergency meeting. The play-house was the natural choice. It was soon clear that our friend needed more than just girlfriends to confide in. We encouraged her to get professional counseling immediately, which she did. She was supported all along by loving friends, and after a lot of work, she and her husband passed through the dark time together to create one of the best relationships I've known.

By 7:45, I was on my way. JoAnn would be readying the play-house for our gathering. It would be twilight as she lit the candles. Twelve candles were always lit for the twelve original Girls' Club members. Although some members have left, and one is no longer with us, we keep their spirits with us, especially at a Playhouse Party. I love to see the candlelight glowing through the windows as the friends begin to arrive. Marilyn usually brings an ice chest with drinks. Linda would bring snacks. A box of tissues was always on the shelf.

I was the last to arrive. They surrounded me with hugs and warm greetings. Refreshments were passed around, and the conversation, though light and friendly, turned to me. And with the weariness JoAnn had sensed on the phone, the words started tumbling out: "I feel overwhelmed. And my family does not seem to understand—or appreciate—all that I am doing to keep it all together."

Everyone knew that my sister Jan's diagnosis of cancer had consumed my thoughts. It was hard to think of anything else, yet I still needed to keep the balance within my own family. A physically demanding job, one teenager struggling at the end of her rebellion, and another just beginning his search for independence made me question my ability to cope. There was a household to run, plus aging parents who deserved my attention as well. It was weighing so heavily that it just felt all too much.

I fought back tears, and a comforting hand reached for my shoulder. There was a stillness in the playhouse. I took a deep breath and went on. "At times, I doubt that I can muster the strength to handle these life situations. Although it seems others may have harder things to face, the weight of my world seems almost unbearable." Someone passed the tissue box.

As my friends listened, I felt comforted by the understanding smiles and expressions of concern. I knew they understood how I felt, some having gone through their own moments of turmoil. It was not necessary for them to say anything or to give advice. It was enough to allow me to share my heartache. That gift alone made the weariness begin to slip away, as their caring replenished my strength.

A Playhouse Party occurs when the need arises. It has become a sanctuary for us to share our thoughts, desires, and troubles. The glow from the playhouse windows is the warmth that comes from the hearts of good friends.

—JILL HENRY'S STORY WRITTEN BY HER SISTER JUDY JULY

"I felt it shelter to speak to you."

—Emily Dickinson

f l o w e r   p o w e r

Your best gal pal's boyfriend just dumped her, and you want to extend a message of support (since you can't actually have him publicly flogged), but cards seem weak and words escape you. Look to those sentimental Victorians for guidance and give her a boost with a blues-busting bouquet.

Following is a veritable garden of blossoms and plants with their various meanings. Inscribe a card to your girlfriend identifying the significance of each bloom to decode your sentiments. For a truly special touch, write the note on parchment, roll it up, and secure it with a pretty ribbon. If fresh flowers aren't practical, give her something with a floral motif that you find particularly meaningful and share the symbolism with her.

blues-busting bouquet

Chrysanthemum: Hope
Freesia: Calmness
Gladiola: Natural grace
Jasmine: Good wishes
Red geranium: Comfort

you lost ten pounds and look like a goddess bouquet

Bird of Paradise: Exotic and wonderful
Delphinium: Swiftness and light
Heather: Passion
Pink flowers: Any variety, the color means perfection

best friends forever bouquet

Forget-me-nots: Keep me in your heart
Periwinkle: Promise
Sunflower: Adoration, strength, longevity
Roses: Love

the language of flowers

Allium: Success, prosperity, good fortune

Almond blossoms: Hope

Amaryllis: Pride or splendor

Aster: Good beginnings

Bachelor Buttons: Singular blessedness or hope

Bird of Paradise: Exotic and wonderful

Camellia: Perfection, excellence

Campanula: Gratitude

Chrysanthemum: Hope; White chrysanthemum: truth; Yellow chrysanthe-mum: slighted love; Red chrysanthemum: "I love"; In China, they signify harvest, rest, and ease

Coreopsis: Always cheerful

Crocus: Youthful joy and gladness

Daffodil: Regard

Dahlia: "You have good taste"

Daisy: White daisy: innocence; Gerbera daisy: purity

Dogwood: Endurance

Forget-me-nots: Keep me in your heart; a Victorian keepsake flower

Gardenia: Grace, artistry

Gladiola: Natural grace, strength of character

Heather: Passion

Heliotrope: Devotion

Hollyhock: Fertility, creation, abundance, ambition

Honeysuckle: Bonds of love and affection

Iris: "I bear a message"

Jasmine: Good luck and increase; White jasmine: amiability; Yellow jasmine: grace and elegance

Laurel: Glory, triumph

Lavender: Renewal and freshness; be careful with this one since its Victorian meaning is distrust

Lilac: Love's first emotions

Lily: White lily: youthful innocence; Middle Eastern tradition touts it as a fertility symbol, Christian symbology aligns it with the Virgin Mary

Magnolia: Love of nature, dignity, perseverance; In the South it means hospitality; In China it symbolizes gentleness and feminine beauty

Orchid: Ecstacy

Pansy: "Thinking of you"

Peony: "I entrust you with a secret," bashfulness; In Japan it signifies prosperity

Peppermint: Warmth of feeling

Petunia: "Do not despair"

Pink flowers: Any variety, the color means perfection

Plumeria: Aloha

Queen Anne's Lace: Self-reliance

Ranunculus: Radiance, charm

Rose: Love; Red rose: deep love; White rose: purity and peace; Red and white together: unity; Yellow rose: jealousy or love of home

Rosemary: Remembrance

Sage: "You are held in high esteem"

Snapdragon: Impetuous

Sunflower: Adoration, power, warmth, nourishment, longevity

Sweet Basil: Good wishes

Sweet Pea: Delicate or lasting pleasure

Tulip: Declaration of love (a Turkish custom)

Violet: Pledge of faithfulness

Zinnia: Thoughts of an absent friend

the Most imPortant FriendshIp

Ours is a lifelong friendship, soul mates. We love the same odd foods, finish each other's sentences, and simultaneously make comments out of the blue. We've always loved the same cartoons that still send us into laughing frenzies. Though I am seven years older than she is, we are so connected to each other that often when I am at my lowest low, crying in grief and wishing she were with me, she magically shows up at my door and soothes my wounds, holding me while I cry or sitting quietly and listening while I ramble through a series of disappointments.

This best friend is my sister Carole. Though we have always adored each other, ours has not always been a smooth friendship. There were many arguments and resentments during our early adult years. Once, at a party, she got so angry she threw a chair at me. At one point I was so furious with her that we didn't talk for about a year. I finally broke the silence when I believed I had found a child to adopt. I wanted her to be a major part of the baby's life. When the adoption didn't work out, she offered to carry my child. If not for the tactical and social challenges, we would have done it. To this day, we both regret not going through with it.

Growing up together generated a lot of great times. Carole always pretended to be the angel child, while I was the rebel. The truth was that we both secretly did things that would have met with great parental disapproval, but we harbored each other's covert activities, making a game out of it. We still laugh about the day I wrote in the fog of the glass shower doors words revealing that my "perfect" sister was sleeping with her boyfriend! I held the shower doors tightly so she couldn't erase them and called my mother in to view the damning message. She tried to erase the words in every possible way, even standing on a chair to reach over the doors, but the doors were too tall. In her panic, she threatened to flush the toilet and scald me. I laughed my head off at her creativity and erased the words. She'd won that game.

We protected each other a lot. I was twenty-one years old when my mother found marijuana in my room. She and my father decided the only right thing to do was to turn me into the authorities. They discussed it for a couple of days and were ready to go through with it until Carole pointed out that if I was convicted of drug possession, I'd have a criminal record and wouldn't be able to find a job and support myself. How clever of her. I glowed with admiration.

On the other hand, after I moved out of our parents' home and got married, she called one night frantically whispering something to me that I couldn't understand. It took me a while to figure out what she was trying to say. It seems she had stashed *her* marijuana under the mattress in my old bedroom. When my mother went to turn the mattresses, she found it and assumed it was Carole's. Thinking on her feet, Carole denied it was hers, and claimed I had left it behind. That's when Carole called me, quietly begging for me to take the blame. What the heck, I figured, they already thought I was a drug abuser, and we didn't have to live under the same roof.

—Nancy Briggin

The Balance of the Road

Occasionally, deep betrayal or living far apart fray girlfriend-hood, but usually it's Friends for Life with women. These are the friendships that last decades, the ones that grow roots and texture and always taste good. When you hear her voice, even over the phone, the bedrock of what you both know about each other pushes all that's real and true to the surface. You can effortlessly soar through all the details of your lives in perfect tandem, switching roles as listener and ranter. Granted, you each have a consistent role, but the dynamics are molten and pliant. Reversible even, given the right circumstances. A different environment is one of those circumstances. Some new, neutral territory.

Traveling with Claire was one of those circumstances.

Claire is spectacular. An astonishing Shakespearean actress, a driven and accomplished athlete, the best writer I know (both prose and poetry), and as smart as the day is long. Power, Grace, and Diana, the goddess of the hunt, personified. Formidable. But silly as can be.

We have this history: junior high sleepovers at her house; surviving brutal 4:00 A.M. bakery shifts on the strength of sheer silliness; bike riding together down icy alleys to keggers; being DJs at the same radio station; and sharing whisky and sociopolitical wisdom as if we'd discovered both. Somewhere in there, she headed to Harvard for a master's at the Divinity School, and I stayed tangled in a long and pointless marriage to a professional poker player.

Claire and I talked often about traveling. I was homesick for the road, and she has a way of talking about adventures (be they future or former) in an epic, romanticized storytelling way that makes you wish you were there. So, we plotted—Claire would take a leave from Harvard and I would leave my husband and we would take the continent of our heritage by storm.

We fully intended to storm country after country like well-fed comets, but jetlag is hell. We finally limped out of London weeks later onto a night train to Paris.

That night was sharp and wild with wind and possibilities. The heartbeat clack of trains coupled with the night air of an open window always does it for me. But Claire was trapped by the whirring of infinite options, none well known. She wanted to make choices by default and familiarity. I wanted to throw myself headlong into the undertow of being on the road.

Suddenly, the superheroine whom I could always watch for the best and bravest moves was hobbled and dependent. I needed to make the decisions and convince her of adventures waiting outside the warmth of a hostel sitting room.

Mind you, there were explosions of escapades: hitchhiking out of the Guinness- and poetry-saturated streets of Dublin north to Giant's Causeway; curled up happily with three generations of Italian women in a sleeper car headed for Florence, and cooking Thanksgiving dinner for a basketball team in Germany with an apple-cheeked grandma who felt Hitler was misunderstood. We witnessed the supernatural howl of an addled and turbaned woman in the 3:00 A.M. french-fry line in the red-light district of Amsterdam and kidnapped an unhappy student in France and carried her off to the

Basque seaside. We shared Christmas mulled-wine visits to Elsinore Castle in Denmark and the pollution-enhanced glow of Athens illuminating the Parthenon.

I can imagine no better companion than Claire for all those exquisite moments, but the balance of our relationship had swung to a new place. I found being the capable one disquieting and awkward. I occasionally shot off to other countries alone, when she needed to burrow and regroup.

But there toward the end, after all the tugging and wobbling of a relationship imbalance, came this night in Greece. A Johnny Walker Red night. An evening of pure lucidity when a crystalline balance was formed without words. We drank in the domestic intimacy of our unpacked bags strewn around the floor, relishing our solidarity against the hostile hostel owner. All the wonderful and strange days we had spent together in the past three months and three decades suddenly distilled in the scotch. In perfect symmetry, Claire and I sipped the strength of our history and imagined all the good things to come.

I hung out of a window tethered by a wire feeling fearless until it snapped and I landed on my head. Claire laughingly measured the lump on my head (golfball?! baseball?!) and there on the floor the balance returned. We came to a scotch-soaked stop of the pendulum swing through all the people we both have been. In that frozen moment we realized we would witness each other's lives unfold with both utter confidence and reverence. A balance was struck, and strung, and has stayed.

—Kris King

sister solidarity

We all know how much fun it is to indulge in female bonding, and we don't know anyone who doesn't wish for more time to hang out with the girls. It's not easy to juggle families, work, relationships, and keep your roots from showing all at the same time. In an effort to spark some connections, we asked women from around the country to share their bonding secrets. So get inspired and hook up.

Before you even begin, legions of chicks agree that you need to set your intention. If there's a friend in your life that you value and treasure, you have to make a true and conscious commitment to make your relationship a priority. We are not the girlfriend police, but nothing happens without effort, so stop making excuses and make some promises you intend to keep.

Send mail. There's nothing better than getting something in the mail with a friendly return address in the upper left corner. Next time you see a pretty card, a postcard, a fun rubber stamp, or even a pretty leaf that your sisterfriend would like—snag it and invest 5 minutes to jot a note and pop it in the mail. This is a quick fix and does not excuse you from real heart-to-heart letter writing or phone calling, but your girlfriend will delight in the gesture.

Date your friends. Why should they be any different than any other love interest? Set a time to hook up, and barring a true emergency (someone's hurt, sick, or dying), keep it. Ratify a "no flaking out" resolution and adhere to it. Maybe you are fortunate enough to live close enough to do dinner, or grab coffee together. Geographic undesirability is no excuse in matters of the heart. If you can't physically meet, set a phone date at an economic long-distance rate time, cozy up on the couch, and have a good old-fashioned gabfest.

Go online. It's a dot.com world, so take advantage of it. E-mail can't surpass more personal communication, but it can keep you abreast of one another's lives, especially when you live far apart. If you have a computer, invest in a modem, and you can get e-mail for free through countless folks. Think of it as a "shared journal" and draft entries to your cyber sister at least once a week to tell her what you've been up to, ask advice, bounce ideas, tell jokes. Cardinal rule: Forwarding stuff is not the same and can *never* replace a personal message.

Coordinate a girlfriend retreat. Rent a cabin, go hiking, luxuriate at a spa, explore a foreign country, or send your kids to Grandma's and take turns hosting at your own homes. The destination is only the beginning of the journey. Coordinating something like this is tough, so be prepared for lots of back and forth, but once you reach consensus on a date and place, stick to it and try to make it an annual event. We know ladies who pay "dues" at their monthly girls' nights and use the money for an annual weekend retreat. If you're spread out around the country, you can individually maintain Buddy Banks and save money for the plane tickets and expenses of converging in one place. Think of all the trouble you can get into. Make a pact: What happens on retreat, stays on retreat!

Long distance relationship? Exchange videotapes of yourselves every few months. Just trade them back and forth, taping over each other's. We know some ladies who have been using the same tape and packaging to exchange messages for three years! This is particularly great if you have kids, since it lets them see their auntie and gives personality to a person they hear about often. Think how fun it would be to actually *show* her your new haircut rather than tell her or send a one-dimensional picture? Hey, this is important stuff.

Wear a badge of friendship. Find a special locket or charm and buy two—one for you and one for her. Wear them as a show of your solidarity. Do something as simple as paint your toenails the same color or exchange your favorite scented candles. Little tokens of friendship and remembrance can keep you in one another's thoughts.

Read the same books. You might already do this, but if not, make a point to start a book club. They are great ways to connect, share your interests, learn about one another's likes and dislikes, expand your literary knowledge, and meet new friends.

Share recipes. Have a new recipe that's scrumptious and the perfect remedy to a bad day? Discovered a breath-taking new dessert that will floor even the dullest dinner guest? So many of us love to bond over food and cooking—share your new discoveries, and encourage your friends to do the same. Or plan a bake night or foodfest where everyone can bring their latest culinary creation.

"It takes a lot of courage to show your dreams to someone else."

—Erma Bombeck

"Whenever I have to choose between two evils, I always like to try the one I haven't tried before."

—Mae West

3

cheeky chicks

Cirque du cHien

The ringmaster appears on stage. He is elegantly dressed in a tuxedo, satin cape, and tall black hat and sports a suave mustache. He announces to the audience, "Bonjour Mesdames et Messieurs! May I introduce to you, Cirque du Chien!" Circus music plays loudly, and the audience applauds as four French poodles come prancing from behind the curtain. The ringmaster introduces each poodle—Fifi, Gigi, Sassy, and Coco. They bow to the audience and yip with excitement at the applause.

The poodles are actually my girlfriends—Lizzie, Carole, Shari—and me. What began as a Halloween costume grew to become a way of life for us for about six months. Shari had the idea of dressing as French poodles for a café party. We immediately loved the idea and spent the next two weekends designing and sewing until we were satisfied that we did indeed look like poodles.

Imagine four women wearing black curly fur headpieces with long floppy ears, matching fur haunches, cuffs, anklets, and tails over black body suits. We each had our own colored bow with coordinating glitter. We weren't just the women who ran with the poodles, we *were* the poodles. We yipped, barked, howled, drank French wine, and smoked French cigarettes, as fun-loving poodles do.

Being poodles for one night was not enough. Somehow, our costumes unleashed hidden talents. We decided to take our show on the road. Calling ourselves "Cirque du Chien," we wrote a script for a 15-minute performance, enlisting Fifi's husband as the ringmaster.

For the show, Gigi was the beatnik poodle and played her saxophone. Sassy was the sentimental poodle and sang a tear-inducing version of "La Vie en Rose." Fifi and Coco performed a very dramatic Apache dance.

The poodles posing for a pic.

That was seven years ago, and we still refer to each other as "the Poodles." Whenever we get together to celebrate a birthday or other event, that close, silly, loving poodle spirit is always there. It's something we've shared that we will never forget. I can see us fifty years from now, Fifi, Gigi, Sassy, and Coco, raising our glasses of wine and toasting, "Vive Le Cirque du Chien!"

—LESA PORCHÉ

tHe ChanTeuse and tHe KentUcKY kiD

Rosemary Clooney met Marlene Dietrich on Tallulah Bankhead's *The Big Show*. It was a rainy night, and while backstage, Rosemary noticed a scruffy figure wearing galoshes and a sloppy raincoat topped with a big scarf shuffle through the back door. Like a butterfly from a cocoon, Marlene emerged from the shabby getup perfectly coifed and elegantly dressed in chiffon and gold. "You sing very well. Now we really should keep in touch, because I think you have a great future," she said to Rosemary, who replied, "I hope you're right. I haven't had a hit yet." Marlene said with assurance, "You will. You will." And thus began a beautiful friendship between the smoky chanteuse and the Kentucky country girl.

In her autobiography, *Girl Singer,* Rosemary Clooney recalls her lifelong friend and how she generously shared advice on everything from how to host an elegant dinner party to the color underwear a woman should sport. "You should wear only underwear that matches your skin, darling." And when she couldn't find the perfect beige, she made strong tea and dyed white panties to her liking. When Rosemary married the divorced José Ferrer, Marlene told her to get rid of the bedroom set his ex-wife had chosen and shop for a new one. "Pick it out and they'll have it in place by tomorrow, because I'll call and tell them," she said.

Marlene would often surprise Rosemary at her performances. A mysterious figure swathed chicly in black, sitting in the first rows, she was always recognizable to Rosemary. When Rosemary had her first baby, Marlene showed up at the hospital with a huge jar of caviar. She cornered the nurse and demanded to know where she kept the penicillin. With a smile she explained, "The temperature at which one keeps penicillin is the perfect temperature for caviar, darling." When Rosemary came down with the flu, Marlene swept into her home, summarily dismissed the maids, donned an apron, and made restorative broth for the girl singer. If she found the floor dirty, she'd get down on her hands and knees and give it a good scrubbing. "You cannot concentrate when you're unwell, darling. The only thing one feels like reading when one is sick is something like this," she'd purr as she handed Rosemary the latest copy of the scandal sheet.

At the height of her affair with Frank Sinatra, Marlene called Rosemary from Las Vegas: "Come up here so we can talk. I can't talk to all these people he surrounds himself with." So Rosemary and her husband answered the summons and went to Vegas. One night at dinner Frank extended an extravagant cigarette case to the table. "That's gorgeous," Rosemary said as Marlene reached for it with a nod to her friend not to

Rosemary and Marlene girltalking.

let on that she'd seen it before. It seems the beautiful jewel-encrusted case was a "standard issue" gift from Marlene to her lovers.

After Marlene's death Rosemary spoke with her daughter Maria Riva about her mother's colorful life and convoluted love affairs, which included numerous men and women. Rosemary remarked that in all the years of their close friendship, Marlene had never made a pass at her, to which Maria replied, "My mother was a perfect gentleman."

"It's the ones you can call up at 4:00 A.M. that matter."

—Marlene Dietrich

Night swimming

I t was midnight when we decided it would be fun to take the motorboat out for a drive. The moon was bright and the stars were out and we were that magical age: sixteen. The three of us had been friends forever. Michigan Betty and I had known each other for more than fifteen years, and Texas Betty and I had met in sailing school when we were twelve. We were the best of summer friends, except when we weren't. Every summer, though, we were together.

This summer was no exception. We arrived at the lake within a week of each other and started meeting on the beach, at the small yacht club, or at the parties that we had every night. This night we were bored. It was the end of the summer season, and we were tired of hiking down to the beach to see the same people every night. We were determined to have a little fun by ourselves. As the engine of our boat roared to life, we decided to go to the beach party anyway, but we'd arrive via the lake.

We navigated the boat slowly through the water, wanting to make a silent approach. We saw the fire and the younger kids gathered around, drinking cheap beer and smoking cigarettes. "What fun," said Michigan Betty, "would it be if we pretended to be the sheriff's patrol?" I found the large flashlight we kept in the boat for emergencies, as well as two smaller ones left over from a night-fishing expedition the week before. We gunned the motor, turned the flashlights toward the party, and started to yell. "Hey, what are you kids doing down here?" "Is that alcohol legal?" "Can you show some ID?"

They started to run, and we laughed. "Okay," said Texas Betty. "Now what?" We sat in the boat, just talking and looking at the stars. Then someone, I'm not sure who, had the great idea to go skinny-dipping. The water was warm and the air was calm, so the three of us took off our clothes and dove in. We shrieked as we hit the water—it was warm, but it was pitch-black, and we couldn't see what our feet kept touching. Mostly it was seaweed, but sometimes our flailing feet hit another flailing foot, which was enough to send us into yelling fits as we imagined the worst sort of sea creatures rising to nibble at our toes and grasp at our legs. We swam around a bit, until the wind began to pick up, and it started to get chilly. I said, "Well, girls, it's been fun, but I am freezing." And I swam up to the boat. And stopped. We had not thought to put the ladder outside the boat (and, in fact, the ladder had been lost the day before). So we had no way of getting back into the boat, except to awkwardly clamber up the side.

So that's what we did.

To get into the boat, you had to throw a leg up over the side. Then, you had to reach a hand to the console that held the steering wheel and pull yourself up into the boat. That is, if you have the arm strength. Texas Betty and I sent Michigan Betty up first. She had good arm muscles and was able to launch herself into the boat. Texas Betty went next, and required a little help. I followed, needing a lot of help. We tried not to look too closely as we each struggled over the side of the boat, but the knowledge that each of us was trying to gracefully climb into the boat, and failing miserably, sent us into fits of laughter.

Michigan Betty started dancing around the boat, swirling her clothes around her head. Texas Betty and I saw the sailboat approaching at the same time and dove for our clothes. The sailboat had a bright light beaming in front of it, to avoid hitting anchored objects. Like us. Michigan Betty did not notice the boat and did not understand our sudden panic. We tried to tell her, but she couldn't make out what we were saying through our laughter. Finally we shouted, *"Boat!"* Her jaw dropped, and she scrambled for her clothes. At that moment, the boat shone its bright spotlight on us . . . right on the backside of Michigan Betty.

Silently, we dressed and docked the boat, carefully avoiding looking at each other until our slow walk back to our houses. Suddenly we looked at each other and laughed until we cried. The next night we went to the beach and listened to story after story from the other kids about how they had all almost gotten caught by the sheriff's patrol the night before.

—Teresa Coronado

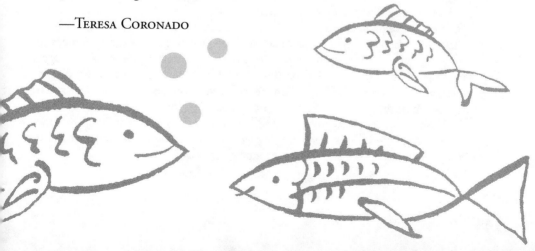

b e a u t y   n i g h t

There's something wonderfully indulgent and—let's face it—fabulously prissy about a bunch of friends fellowshipping in the name of toenail painting, facial masking, and manicuring. Perhaps it's the old-fashioned power of connecting with your inner glamour-puss or simply the sheer chickcentricity of giggling over a foofy libation. No matter your beauty style, a night of feminine indulgence is a powerful bonding ritual. Who can be self-conscious or aloof while sporting a mask of green gooey mud?

For a true dose of girl power, host a good ol'-fashioned beauty parlor night. The gal on the go can find kits that are literally parties in a can. Two of our favorites are Beauty Parlor Night Kit, by TomGirls and Spa-Dada Facial Expression Kit, by Deserving Thyme.

A less expensive way is to send out an invitation and elect each person to bring an item or share a secret beauty potion. Or you can support a local gal's mission to drive that pink Cadillac by calling on a Mary Kay consultant or other trained professional. Be sure to have lots of clean towels on hand, plastic tubs for foot soaking, cotton balls, cotton swabs, and beauty basics like nail polish remover, headbands, and moisturizer.

Don't forget the food and drink. Go spa-inspired with pitchers of spring water with floating cucumber slices and fruit or make white wine spritzers. For food, think bite-sized snacks such as sliced fruits, crackers, and dips. Set a relaxed mood with candles, music, and lots of comfy pillows for reclining and lolling about. Pop *Steel Magnolias* in the VCR and pretend you're all at Truvy's.

If makeup and skin care aren't your bag, how about an aromatherapy night, where you share your favorite scent blends and catch up over a glass of wine? *Seasons of Aromatherapy*, by Judith Fitzsimmons and Paula Bousquet, is a beautiful book that provides recipes, lore, and inspiration on the art of aromatherapy. As hostess with the mostest you can provide the "base" for scent-sational goodies by purchasing travel-sized plastic bottles and filling them with an unscented lotion from the drugstore. Get stick-on labels from the office supply store so that you can write down the recipes and label the bottles. For a parting gift, inscribe a couple of concoctions on a little piece of parchment and tie it with a pretty ribbon.

These are two of our favorites from *Seasons of Aromatherapy* (we "chickified" the titles):

Let Him Kiss Your Hands *and* Feet Cuticle Conditioner

2 drops geranium essential oil
4 drops clary sage essential oil
4 drops lavender essential oil
2 drops rosemary essential oil
1 tablespoon sweet almond oil
1/2 teaspoon castor oil

Combine the sweet almond oil and castor oil with the fragrances. Rub this mixture into your cuticles before bedtime every night.

Road to Shangri-La Perfume Oil

3 drops Jasmine
1 drop Sandalwood
1 drop Clary Sage

Mix together and dot on your pulse points for a sensual signature fragrance.

"A woman who doesn't wear perfume has no future." —Coco Chanel

b e a s t   n i g h t

We've all had moments when we would rather shave our heads than take the time to carefully coif and blow-dry our hair, and the idea of a beauty parlor night when you feel like a troll might be tough to swallow. So, as an alternative to beautification, how about beastification?!

Here is a formula for a debaucherous, all-you-can-eat, late night chickfest:

Your Garb: All the clothes your mother hates to see you in—your ratty jeans, stained sweats, and old shoes

Makeup: None, or just enough so the fire department won't think you're a corpse if they show up

The Crowd: All your best gals (leaving out the ones who never have a bad hair day or those who never pig out)

The Decor: Your apartment strewn with pillows and plenty of spots to dump food and drinks

The Pig Out: Think salt and sugar—Velveeta® salsa cheese dip with tortilla chips, brie, salsa, chocolate dipping sauce and plenty of strawberries, s'mores (melt the marshmallows in the microwave and use the chocolate dipping sauce), chocolate chip cookie dough, and ice cream!

The Libations: Soda, wine, beer, and martinis

The Festivities: Paint your toenails black, crank call all your ex-boyfriends, and watch *Thelma and Louise*

The Gab: Everything from guys and politics to body hair and career advancement

Soundtrack: Pat Benatar, The Dixie Chicks, Sister Sledge, Gloria Gaynor, Carole King, Indigo Girls

To get you started, here are a few of our Beast Night favorites.

Loopy Laura Martinis

Absolute Currant
Pink lemonade
Squeeze of fresh lemon

Mix this up until it's yummy (about 1 part vodka to 3 parts lemonade is a good start.) Take everyone's keys at the door. This cocktail makes your gathering an automatic slumber party. If you don't believe us, ask Laura.

Velveeta® Salsa Cheese Dip

1 1/2 lbs. (24 oz.) Velveeta® cheese spread cut into chunks
1 1/2 cups of salsa

Combine cheese and salsa in a 2 1/2-quart microwavable bowl and cook on high for 4 minutes; stir. Microwave 2 minutes on high and stir again. Repeat the 2 minute bursts and stir until the cheese is melted and creamy. Serve with tortilla chips and pretzels. Serves 24—36.

Chocolate Sinful Sauce

6 ounces semisweet chocolate chips
1/2 cup light cream
2 tablespoons Kirsh or Grand Marnier

Melt the chips in a double boiler over boiling water. Add the cream and Kirsh or Grand Marnier and blend well. Keep warm when serving. You could dip anything in here and it would taste good. Fruit (if you must), peanuts, graham crackers smeared with peanut butter, marshmallows, popcorn.

"Never eat more than you can carry."

—Miss Piggy

The sWeet PoTatO Queens

Our most memorable trip ever was a trip to Graceland. One of the Queens, Tammy, had a guy friend who was coming to visit her, and for some reason he needed to be picked up in Memphis. So what we did, as if it made perfect sense, was to rent a big old tour bus. A real one, like the ones rock stars use on the road. We rented it for the day and went to Memphis in it. . . .

We were on our way to Memphis on the bus. Tammy had told her friend just to go to Graceland and wait for his ride. "You'll be picked up" is all she had said. All the way to Memphis, we tried on trashy lingerie. Everybody brought every article of pretty ditties she owned, and we tried them all on in every possible combination, selecting just the right thing to wear to Graceland. Even though Elvis would not actually be there, we wanted to dress appropriately. We decided that Tammy's high heels weren't high enough, and so when we got to Memphis a little early, we went in search of spikes for her. We happened to be in a neighborhood of Memphis that was filled with pawnshops. The sight of all those pawnshops got Tammy to thinking about handcuffs—the Queens love handcuffs—and soon everybody was clamoring for handcuffs. We stopped at a number of pawnshops and went in, wearing our carefully selected outfits under our fur coats. Nobody had handcuffs. All they had was some of the very biggest gold chains we'd ever seen. I don't think those chains exist anywhere outside of pawnshops—pawnshops in Memphis, for that matter. Handcuffless, we continued the search for

Her Royal Highnesses, The Sweet Potato Queens.

trashy shoes for Tammy. You just can't wear a sensible midheel with a black lace teddy. It contradicts the whole look. We finally found what we wanted. Then on to Graceland.

As we pulled into the parking lot of the souvenir mall across the street from Graceland, we sighted Tammy's guy, standing on the corner with his suitcase, watching the cars whiz by. He never so much as glanced at our bus, so totally unsuspecting was he that it was ours. We rumbled into the parking lot and debarked. As we strode across the parking lot with our high heels clicking on the pavement, we shrugged off our fur coats—despite the frosty wind—to reveal our outfits: black high heels, black tights, and black lace teddies. We looked like we'd escaped from a Robert Palmer "Addicted to Love" recording session. Tammy's fellow followed the gaze of the quickly accumulating crowd in the parking lot, and his little face just lit right up when he saw us. He seemed genuinely glad to see us. I guess the reasons were obvious: partly because he was freezing and sick of standing on the corner waiting for a ride, and partly because there was a whole big gang of women from Mississippi in black lace underwear walking across the parking lot with half of Memphis slamming on the brakes to gawk at them—and they were there to meet him. I believe he walked a little taller that day.

—JILL CONNER BROWNE, THE SWEET POTATO QUEEN

"If you don't have *Real Live Majorette Boots* at this stage in your life, it's your own [damn] fault. Quit whining and go out and get some!"

—Jill Conner Browne, The Sweet Potato Queen

The Fun Bunch goes jammin'

"The Fun Bunch" came together in New York City in the late '80s. We were living in college dorms—eight chicks, representing seven states, many different accents, and one hairstyle: BIG.

Jill had the biggest hair, hands down. She was a nice Jewish girl from Connecticut, but she could make her curly locks explode. She'd stack her tools in front of her—blow-dryer, 17-inch can of hairspray, massive hairbrush—and go to work. We would all stand back in awe as she worked her magic.

We each had our talents for hitting the town. Tracy was the "dresser"—she could put an ensemble together in 5 seconds flat. She never used a clothes hanger in her life, but out of her piles, she could stylishly outfit all eight of us. Jody always provided the music, because she had the best stereo; Kim, the spirit, because she could inevitably recite thirteen reasons why we needed to celebrate that very minute. Amy came up with the when, where, and why, because she was the most reasonable; Terry's innocence lent an air of optimism; Elisabeth brought the jelly doughnuts, m&ms™, and international expertise, and I brought up the rear, in case there were any stragglers.

Over the years the Fun Bunch had developed certain rules about going out, and now that we were seniors, they were part and parcel of our outings:

chick schtick

Every group of gals has some priceless expression all its own—part code, part slang—that creeps into its vocabulary when its members are together. We've interviewed some of our favorite girlfriend gangs for these fabulously fun words and phrases—spread them around!

Bunk: Used to describe something negative, a bummer: "Working late, what a load of bunk!"

God love her *and* Bless her heart: Every Southern belle knows that you can say anything if you begin it with one of these magic phrases: "God love him, he's bald as a cue ball." "Bless her heart, she's so bucktoothed she could eat apples through a fence."

I bet he can dance: A lustful comment used to describe a sexy guy.

If I were a guy . . .: A compliment you give your girlfriends when they're all dolled up and ready for a night on the town: "Honey, if I were a guy!"

Lipping up: Applying lipstick.

Must have: Perfectly expresses that lack of self-control we all confront every once in a while. It can apply to anything from a pair of shoes to a good-looking man.

MYOB: Mind your own business.

Ohmigod: Used to add emphasis at the beginning of a sentence at a moment of excitement: "Ohmigod. Did he really say that????" or "Ohmigod. Cute shoes!!!!!"

Petite fleur: An expression used to describe yourself as you are standing in line for a

1. Have big hair—and lots of it.

2. Never set out before 10:30 P.M.

3. Be sure to arrive slightly—if not very—intoxicated.

4. Dominate the scene by singing as loudly as possible.

One of the most anticipated events of our senior year was the spring-break trip to Jamaica. Despite the absurdly cheap "package" deal arranged for us by a fellow collegian (who later became my adored husband), we convinced ourselves that we were staying in a resort that would pale the Ritz by comparison.

We left New York City with beastly hangovers on a frigid March morning and boarded an Air Jamaica

• • •

third piece of cheesecake: "I know I'm just a *petite fleur,* but I *need* another piece *now.*"

Squirrel: An undesirable man.

Sweet victory: An expression of great triumph or satisfaction. Equally effective whether yelled out or said casually.

Talk to the hand: An utterly smart-alecky remark used when someone is saying something very disagreeable (like dissing your girlfriend). Interrupt the person, hold out your hand, and turn your face away. A fierce look of disgust makes this even more potent.

TMI: Too much information.

WOOMAAN!: A cheer of success or great jubilation. This exclamation is particularly irksome to certain types of men.

plane that had big brown and green flowers on the seats. Even the hellish bus ride at 70 miles per hour on a winding narrow road couldn't dampen our spirits. When we finally arrived at our hotel, the Pink Flamingo, it was painfully obvious, even from the dank interior of the bus, that not only would it never be mistaken for the Ritz, but, to put it nicely, it was still under construction. Elisabeth reminded us that we were now in a third world country—and that many of its residents didn't even have running water. So we quickly devised the Jamaica party-going rules:

1. Jamaican (Bo Derek wannabe) cornrows are enhanced by unwashed hair.

2. Stay as dehydrated as possible to avoid the bathrooms.

3. Keep Jack Daniels around—it doesn't need refrigeration, makes a pretty good mosquito repellant, and kills germs.

Activity or movement was strongly discouraged during our days in Jamaica—we had to rest up for our nightly escapades, plus too much stirring around might make us thirsty (remember rule #2!). However, feeling unusually energetic one day, Kim and I took inflatable rafts out for a relaxing float. As we drifted farther and farther from the beach and the water got deeper and more shadowy, we started talking about shark attacks and became so overcome by fish phobia that we fell off our rafts. The rafts were narrow, and in the deep water, we were unable to get back on them. We wore ourselves out laughing hysterically while shrieking and struggling to get back on the rafts. As exhaustion set in, we gave up and settled for getting our torsos on the rafts and letting our limbs dangle in the water.

"Not too much flailing," Kim reminded me, "or we'll attract more sharks."

Slowly, we swam back to the beach where we could see our friends enjoying frozen drinks while safely ensconced on the white sand. When we finally hit shore, we were about a quarter of a mile from the rest of the Fun Bunch and had to make our way through a maze of sunbathing Jamaicans who seemed a bit too enthusiastic about our return. As we met with stares and catcalls, I remember thinking that perhaps they had all noticed our struggle and were happy for our safe return. As we got closer to our friends, I heard Amy crying, "Kim! Kim!" and saw her making frantic hand motions around her bathing suit top. Our other friends just stared with horrified expressions on their faces, and Terry fell facedown into her towel laughing. When we got close enough to hear Amy clearly, we realized what she had failed to communicate was that Kim's bikini top was completely twisted around her body, leaving her chest totally naked!

Kim was furious. On top of surviving the raft journey from hell, where we'd deluded ourselves into believing that we were almost eaten by hungry sharks, and losing God knows how many dirty corn-rows at 50 cents a pop in our battle with the floats, she had flashed every lecherous onlooker on the beach. She was dissatisfied with Amy's efforts to warn her and complained bitterly about her "ineffective and cryptic hand motions" for days. We weren't even allowed to mention the Great Naked Beach Walk until we returned to New York City. (Where it quickly became legend!)

Our day of greatest exposure, however, came while visiting what we believed to be a very posh bar set on the cliffs near Negril, where the sunset was gorgeous and enthusiastic people jump off the cliffs into a small cove. Cheering boisterously for each other, we all tried it—one after another—lapping up the hoots and hollers from our comrades before smacking into the shining Jamaican water 30 feet below. Bathing suit recovery was a big issue though, and we needed our sisterfriends' advice on coverage before exiting the water among the throngs of eager men who were standing along the cliffs. But modesty was thrown to the wind when Tracy decided to jump. Slowly, she walked along the cliff contemplating her jump. We all cheered for her from the edge. She seemed to be taking a lot longer than usual, and I began to get concerned that she was contemplating backing out. Just when I thought a rescue was in order, Tracy ripped off her bikini and jumped in. We all lost our voices that night from the yelling.

—EMILY MILES TERRY

Disco *baBes*

When I was a college girl in Boston, my partner in crime and all fun endeavors was Anna. She was a petite bombshell with lovely dark skin and beautiful brown eyes that sparkled with mischief. She was Raquel Welch to my Sandra Dee. We were nineteen at the time, but she was never tagged as less than a worldly twenty-five. I, on the other hand, got mistaken on a daily basis for a fifteen-year-old Catholic schoolgirl. Anna was an Italian princess, and since *Saturday Night Fever* was hot at the box office, she was always on the lookout for her very own John Travolta.

Early in our partnership, we christened ourselves "the Disco Babes." It was the '70s, and we were born at the right time. There was nothing we loved more than glamming up and hitting the Metro in downtown Boston for drinks, dancing, and sundry nightlife antics. To say that we were short on funds would be a great understatement, but the dire state of our bank accounts only fueled our creativity for concocting adventures on a shoestring. We were the queens of budget barhopping.

Short of funds but long on style, we developed a way to satisfy both needs—we "borrowed" dresses and took them for test drives. We'd tromp down to Jordan Marsh, where we'd peruse the racks for anything black, tight, and short in the skirt. Hours later, exhausted from shimmying into dress after dress and critiquing each other mercilessly, we'd ring up our ticket to the nightlife and head home. We'd take the dress out, show it a good time, and invest a great deal of time trying not to sweat in it and protecting it from sloppy drinkers and smoke-filled rooms. After a long night, we'd arrive home, carefully extract the pinned-down tags, hang the frocks outside to air on our fire escape, and pray to find them pristine and odor-free in the morning, when they'd return to their boring life at the mall.

One day, after spending a particularly successful afternoon shopping, Anna and I begged our friend Linda to lend us her red Firebird for the night—we'd scored particularly short dresses and wanted to roll up in style. When Linda wouldn't relent, we moped, saw her off on a date, and dressed up anyway. She'd left the shiny keys on the table, and we decided that since she put them in such a prominent place, surely she'd changed her mind at the last minute, and who were we to refuse her generosity? She'd also left her driver's license. Another act of charity, since I was underage and often relied on her ID to gain entrance into bars and discos. No one seemed to care that I was a petite Irish girl who needed dangerously high pumps to reach a 5'4" stature and Linda was a towering 5'11" and Italian. Anna and I spritzed our hair again, squirted our wrists with one more mist of Charlie, and hit the road. With "I Love the Night Life" blasting, we were ready for a rocking night on the town.

The red car and short skirts got us past the velvet rope and into the pulsing core of the Metro. We'd already spent esteem-boosting time staring in the mirror and repeatedly saying, "We look good. Who could look better than us?" Both brunettes, the answer that haunted our "Who looks better than us?" query was always "A blonde." If Superman met his weakness in the form of cryptonite, our nemesis was any woman with blonde hair. It was especially true this evening. Blondes ruled the Metro, and no matter how homely their features, their chemically enhanced tresses always seemed to attract the spotlight. Anna and I felt defenseless in the glare of their shining locks. "Look out," Anna spent the evening saying, "a Farrah at three o'clock." We'd check her out and always discern that if she were brunette, she'd be downright plain. Damn peroxide and every woman with the courage to put it on her head.

Since we'd invested our meager funds on filling the gas tank of the Firebird, we spent the evening ordering water, getting dirty looks from the bartenders, and debating how the brunettes would look as blondes while we danced wildly together with our arms out to keep from sweating. It doesn't cost a thing to dance, so with "Play That Funky Music, White Boy" and "Funky Town" setting the stage, we created our very own disco inferno. The pinnacle of the night came when the DJ played another of our favorite tunes, "San Francisco," by the Village People, and everyone formed a circle

the shirt off her back

Sharon Stone met Mimi Craven on the set of *Deadly Blessings,* a movie Sharon appeared in that was directed by Mimi's husband, Wes. While the first part of the movie's title is apropos in terms of box office success, the latter describes the start of a phenomenal female friendship. In a 1998 interview, Mimi told a story about how she was feeling really down one day when Sharon came by for a lunch date. After Mimi told Sharon she wasn't feeling well, Sharon looked at her and said assuredly, "It's what you're wearing." She proceeded to pull her own shirt up over her head and hand it to Mimi. Mimi put it on, gave Sharon one of hers, and they headed out. Mimi said, "She was right. I did feel better in her shirt."

and took turns dancing and posing in the middle.

Thankfully, we beat Linda home, placed the keys in the spot where we had found them, and scanned our dresses for damage. Like Cinderellas after the ball, we recapped the night. After hanging our dresses out, we hit our pillows and fell asleep discussing what shade of blonde would be best for each of us. We woke up the next morning to discover it had been a damp night followed by a very cold morning and our dresses were frozen stiff! We laughed until we cried, because, well, what else could we do?

—LORIN FLYNN-BELL

"There are shortcuts to happiness, and dancing is one of them."
—Vicki Baum

HeLL's bElles

A group of us created a club we called "Hell's Belles," jokingly patterned after the Hell's Angels. It was just bunch of overgrown girls with mopeds, but we thought we were every bit as bad as the originals. The charter members were Judy, me, Colleen, Cassie, and Colleen's friend Margaret Hickle, who had come down from Knoxville to help Colleen with her children and to do my housecleaning.

Colleen sewed really well, so she made outfits for all of us. I bought the mopeds in all colors, and we were off to terrorize the back streets of Nashville. One day we were out on the streets, in a competitive mood, and decided to race to see who could be the first one back to my driveway. Each "Belle" took off on what she thought was the fastest way back to my house. I went down one street, and Colleen took another. We got to the house at the same time, but from different directions. I tore across the front yard, trying to get the jump on Colleen. She took a different angle toward the same destination. With our eyes more on

Dolly, leader of the pack.

our goal than each other, we crashed together, then into the same tree.

We were both bruised, burned from the exhaust pipes, scratched and scraped, but laughing to beat the band. Judy and Margaret came along and picked up what was left of us. Colleen had sprained her wrist. Since she was a hairdresser, that was an unfortunate injury for her. I had scratched my face, and since I was on TV, that was about the worst thing I could have done. That was the end of the gang, at least as far as the mopeds were concerned.

—DOLLY PARTON

"I'm not going to limit myself just because people won't accept the fact that I can do something else."

—Dolly Parton

La bella Mafia

La Bella Mafia is a motley crew of characters who found one another in a roundabout way, most of us having worked together at one point or another. We began to coalesce when a group of us started our weekly Girls' Night. At first, it was an excuse to visit my ex-boyfriend at his job at a pizza parlor, but it quickly became an integral part of our week and our friendships. Heck, after a certain point my old boyfriend didn't even have to be working on the night we visited, and eventually we skipped the pizza altogether and went out simply for the friendship, the laughter, the planning of our social calendar, and, of course, the beer.

Fanny always drives, and once we get onto the highway and successfully complete the four-lane glide into the carpool lane *(Sweet victory!)*, Krinnie, who always sits in the front 'cause she gets carsick, begins the routine. She digs into Fanny's glove compartment and pulls out the nuns. That's right, the nuns—tiny plastic black and white nun finger puppets. She doles them out to Marie, Wiwwa, and me, sitting in the back seat, and we begin to sing, at the tops of our voices: "HOW DO YOU SOLVE A PROBLEM LIKE MAA-REEE-AAA!"

Somehow, the ride just flies by.

A lot of our conversations start out "You know what I love about us?" because none of us had ever found all the things we were looking for in a friendship with so many people all at one time. I mean, sure, we've all had good friends before, but we fully believe that there is some sort of divine providence that brought us all here together, at one time, in one place, and all ready to explore grown-up friendships with other women.

LBM on their regular girls' night out.

We aren't the same, by any means, but we do think an awful lot alike. We value respect and understanding, but also fun and silliness and adventure and spontaneity and hugs and laughter. We know that at least one girl will be with us for any trial or event or road trip or funk or crying jag or whining session, and that the others, if they aren't there already, are on their way. At one time or another, each of us has played the role required of us—be it buddy, mother, sister, partner in crime, or shoulder to cry on. Or all at once, if need be.

We aren't afraid to be dorks in public. Really. We sing "Maria" loudly and badly. We talk into our beers pretending they're microphones. We overdress for every occasion, and shout out our joys, and less often, our woes, for anyone to hear.

Like all groups of fabulous, glorious divas, we have our share of admirers at clubs and bars and sometimes we have to go to great lengths to encourage them to leave us alone or, at the very least, to stop gawking....

One Fourth of July, La Bella Mafia traveled to San Jose's festive celebration in Guadalupe Park. As we were taking in the sights, we were rudely accosted by a person who could be described as a "religious fanatic." Now, LBM is not in any way opposed to religion, in fact a few of us are quite intrigued by subjects of a religious nature, but we also believe in a strong female spirit. Rather than engage in a stimulating discussion, this gentleman preferred to shove his beliefs down our throats and ignore our opinions. This offended us.

After that experience we concluded that we needed an international symbol for such situations. One that would truly express, without words, our absolute disinterest in the matter at hand, and our disgust at the manner with which we were being treated, and leave a parting comment on the offending subject's behavior.

And that's when Marie came up with the Group Moon.

Later in the summer, La Bella Mafia took a group trip to Washington State to visit Wiwwa's mom. We were the first people at the airport, and the last ones on the plane, and we all dressed in matching Hawaiian print pajama pants.

Beers were only $2 on the plane.

At the airport we were picked up by a longtime friend of Wiwwa's. Her name is Mac, and as she greeted us by name despite never having met any of us before, we knew she was "in." And we told her so. Often.

So we started our whirlwind tour of Spokane, heading straight from the airport to one of Mac's favorite bars. Course, we were all a little punch drunk (okay maybe just drunk; remember, beers were only $2 on the plane!), and we were being our boisterous, outgoing, loud selves. Some people might say obnoxious. We say vivacious. Anyway, Mac was joining in, laughing, and watching the other folks in the bar watch us, and told us, "I don't think this place has ever seen anything like you guys before!" No, that didn't encourage us at all! Eventually, a couple of members of the opposite sex came over to bother, I mean, talk to us.

Anyway, to make a long story even longer, one of the guys started becoming belligerent. It may have been because we told him we were a Hawaiian karate troupe on vacation. At any rate, he was being a jerk, and his friends hurried him out the door. Little did we know he would be lurking on the sidewalk when we left. Casual insults were exchanged.

Creep: "Why don't you guys just beat it?"

Mac: "Who are you,

the best of the chick tunes

Most girlfriend groups have an insatiable desire to bellow select tunes together—especially when driving in our cars or sitting on our barstools. Occasionally we all need to heed the call of the inner diva/dancing queen.

"Respect," by Aretha Franklin—The Mother of all chick tunes, words to live by!

"Girls Just Wanna Have Fun," by Cyndi Lauper—Nobody can be-bop like a girlfriend gang.

"No Scrubs," by TLC—A "back off, boys" ballad.

"Goodby Earl," by The Dixie Chicks—A bad dude messes with the wrong chicks.

"Girls with Guitars," by Wynonna—The air guitar song supreme.

"I Will Survive," by Gloria Gaynor—A drama queen's dream. Belt it out with your head held high.

"Our Lips Are Sealed," by the Go-Go's—We like to pretend that the men don't get the double entendre.

"We Are Family," by Sister Sledge—Best sung when everyone is standing with arms around shoulders.

"What's Love Got to Do with It?" by Tina Turner—Yell the "Oh-oh" part.

"Man, I Feel Like a Woman," by Shania Twain—A rocking girl's night out anthem.

Michael Jackson?" (moonwalking—really!)

But despite our superior wit and Mac's amazing dance skills, it was obvious that drastic measures were needed.

I don't remember who shouted it first, or whose hands first went to the elasticized waist of those now incredibly convenient pajama pants, or if poor Mac even got her belt undone, but I do remember the way our battle cry grew strong and echoed through the streets of Spokane: "GROUP MOON!"

And it was good.

—Jen Buck

"Clarice, you are too twisted for color TV. *Have your roots done.*"

—Ouiser in *Steel Magnolias*

Joy riDe

During my freshman year in high school, I made friends with a new girl who had just moved to town. Since we had moved nine times before I was twelve, I felt an obligation to take new kids under my wing. Carrie was cute, had a wicked sense of humor and a singing voice like Joni Mitchell. There was also a side to her that seemed old beyond her years and a little mysterious.

The first time I spent the night at her house, I learned why. Her parents had a strange marriage, one that seemed to be mired in separateness, and as her mother sat chain-smoking in the kitchen complaining about her husband's girlfriend, I sensed that she was relieved to see her daughter with a fairly normal friend. I had the required combination of acne, bad fashion, and respect for elders—so I guess I was your typical don't-you-wish-you-were-me teen.

It was a Friday night, and we were fourteen, so our options were pretty limited. Movies were out. Parties were out; we were a hair too young. And there was no football game or school dance. So we sat playing cards, smelling perfume samples, doing face masks, trying to figure out who we were.

Carrie had other plans, though. And as soon as her mother went to bed, she announced them. "Let's sneak the car out and go for a drive!" I was game. "And you can drive," she added. Carrie didn't know how to drive, and since I had driven once before, it seemed best that someone experienced take the challenge. I was fourteen and a half.

Grabbing the keys off the kitchen counter at about 10:00 P.M., we hustled out the door. "It should be easy to drive," Carrie, the rookie, exclaimed. "It's a Mercedes."

So there I was, silently rolling in reverse, down the driveway, which was on a hill, with the engine off, in a car that had power steering. Now we adults know what happens when you try to turn the wheel with power steering. *It doesn't turn.* So, instead of making a clean, quiet getaway, I ran over their Japanese maple, went through their rock garden, and got stuck on a large boulder. Two wheels were off the ground, spinning, and we were completely freaking out. Not only was the car stuck, but we'd just produced some major noise. We sat in the car for several minutes, waiting for Carrie's mother to turn the lights on and catch us red-handed. I was contemplating what excuse I would give my father.

To our astonished, permed-hair selves, nobody woke up. We timidly got out of the car and realized that even if we started the engine, the wheels were off the ground. We needed help. So, summoning up the marathon runner within, we booked three miles to the local hamburger joint. Lucky for us, three large senior football players were finishing up their burgers. They found our story amusing and offered to help. They drove us back to Carrie's house, and then one of them got in the car and turned on the engine, while the other two pushed the car up off the rock. The noise was explosive, and I was grateful for the sleeping pills and Valium that Carrie's mother had to have taken in order to sleep through our escape.

We were home free! The car was off the rocks, we hadn't been busted, and I was beginning to feel the thrill of doing something scandalous and getting away with it. We drove the car for 300 miles, until 4:00 A.M. We didn't do anything specific, just drove. We looked for parties. We drove by the houses of boys that we liked. We got on the freeway. We went to a 7–11 for candy bars. We ran the gas tank down to empty and just made it back to Carrie's.

The night was a success. I discovered the adrenaline you get from breaking the rules. It was the start of my high school career of sneaking out windows, off campus, and into cars. Carrie and I continued to wreak havoc, albeit on the sly. And now, a wiser thirty-one years old, I have a sweet baby girl who is sure to avenge my parents some day.

—KAREN BOURIS NEWTON

"Let's keep going. GO!"
—Thelma in *Thelma and Louise*

Run like hell

Kyra and I are both Aries. We became friends in fifth grade when I transferred schools. She is Irish. I am Cuban. It was a Lucy-Ricky type of relationship. Lots of funny situations and crazy miscommunications.

The first summer we knew each other, on a sunny afternoon, Kyra came to my house and we decided to sell lemonade. We were very excited about the entrepreneurial zeal behind a lemonade stand and the freedom to sit on the street all day and talk to whoever walked by. With a warning about strangers, my mom let us use her nice glass pitcher and allowed us to take a small folding table and chairs outside. We nodded and smiled, pretended to listen, and then ran outside.

Because traffic near my house was slow, we took our makeshift business to the corner of the street and tried to sell there. Not one car passed by, and slowly we drained the pitcher ourselves.

We were ready to close shop after two hours with barely a glass of lemonade left to sell, when a car slowed down. An adolescent male peered out and asked for a glass. We looked at each other and back at him dumbfounded. He was a teenager! He asked again, and we still stared blankly. Two more heads peered out of the gargantuan vehicle.

We looked at each other, got up out of our seats, grabbed each other's hands, and fled straight into my house, leaving behind my mom's glass pitcher, the table, the chairs, and the cup with change that we never had to use. Our hearts were pounding and after I slammed the door shut, we stared at each other. Then we burst out laughing. We didn't know why we ran away from our one and only customer or why we had been dumbfounded in the first place. It was a knee-jerk reaction to being approached by someone strange. I guess we had been listening to my mom after all.

—CRISTINA T. LOPEZ

test your chick quotient

"To have good friends, you gotta be a good friend." If your mother didn't tell you this, consider yourself notified and be grateful you have any buddies to speak of. Or maybe you already know what it takes to be a chick's best friend and have the girlfriend gang to prove it. Regardless, it never hurts to hone up on your CQ—Chick Quotient. Take the test below to see how your friendship abilities rate.

1. You get a call from a girlfriend at work while your boss is sitting in your office. She is obviously very upset. Truly upset, not some drama queen indulgence. Do you

   a. Tell her you have someone in your office, you can't really talk and you'll call her back?

   b. Cover the receiver, tell your boss that this is a very important call, and ask if she can excuse you for a few minutes while you take it?

2. Your girlfriend has not returned your calls after you've left her two messages. Do you

   a. Feel hurt and wait for her to call you back?

   b. Call her again and tell her you miss her?

3. You're doing a mall stomp, and your best friend tries on a slinky velvet number that makes her look like a Polish kielbasa, and she (gulp) loves it. Do you

   a. Smile and say she looks great?

   b. Tell her the outfit would make Kate Moss look bloated, and she should forego it?

4. Your girlfriend's date repeatedly brushes against you and boldly grabs your behind. Do you

   a. Take him aside and tell him what a louse he is, but save your girlfriend the embarrassment?

   b. Feign something is in your eye, take your friend aside and tell her the guy's a creep?

5. Your girlfriend gives you a truly horrible scarf for your birthday. Do you

   a. Tell her flat out it's not you and ask if you can return it?

   b. Wear it fondly when she's around?

6. She's found the man of her dreams; you think she must be hallucinating. Do you

   a. Take every opportunity to point out their differences and highlight his shortcomings?

   b. Support her choices and practically bite through your own tongue around the bozo?

7. You're on a girlfriend getaway, and your road sister keeps using your shampoo, and your conditioner, and your lotion, and your razor, and your hair dryer... Do you

   a. Get up extra early to avoid the battle of the blow-dryer, then pack everything away?

   b. Say, "Hey, what do I look like, your mother?" and share with her anyway.

8. She's had one margarita too many and begins to tango quite clumsily but lustily with a lounge lizard. Do you

a. Cheer them on and order another round?

b. Grab her by the ear and tell Godzilla she's got someplace to be?

9. Your sisterfriend takes up with a crowd that makes you uneasy. Do you

a. Tell her flat out you think they are losers and she has to choose?

b. Tag along from time to time and get your digs in when you can?

10. She forgets your birthday. Do you

a. Vow to "forget" hers and harbor a hurt?

b. Call her up and say, "Hey, did you forget something?"

the results:

Mostly "a" answers: Go straight to the Girlfriend Hall of Shame and read the stories in this book five times each. You make Nellie Olson look like a great best friend.

Mostly "b" answers: You got it goin' on, sister, and you probably have a gaggle of die-hard chick friends to prove it. Consult pages 102–105 for inspiration, and host a girls' night to celebrate.

Half and half: There's hope. You have what it takes but you just get a little stuck sometimes. Rule of thumb: Follow your heart and consider what the best move is to support your girlfriends and foster their success and happiness. You can't go wrong with that.

"Fear less, hope more; eat less, chew more; whine less, breathe more; talk less, say more; love more, and all good things will be yours."

—Swedish Proverb

"If you want something said,
ask a man.
If you want something done,
ask a woman."

—Margaret Thatcher

4

chicks in charge

Capricious Capricorns

My older sister was working for Miss G. [Ava Gardner] around the time she was married to Artie Shaw. When my sister found she had to go back to Chicago, she said, "Reenie, why don't you work for Ava? She's such a sweet little girl and she needs somebody that she can trust. She's going through some terrible times."

I began working for Miss G. in 1947 or 1948 and we were just pals from day one. We could get mad at one another, but we never stopped speaking. All these years, whether we were together or not, that was the one thing we had. I guess that's why we remained friends. She was fun, and very sharing. If I ever made her anything from a cup of coffee to a martini, she'd say, "Well, where's yours?" She wasn't what we thought of as the stereotypical Southerner. We'd go to clubs during the time before integration, and if they threw me out, she'd leave too. So to keep her, they'd tolerate me. We were both Capricorns, and Capricorns just work with the present. Sometimes I'd wake her up and she'd say, "Oh shit, what's today gonna bring?"

Her work was, as she would say, a paycheck. She knew this was the only work she could do where she could make a decent living, and she'd say, "If you can get me there, Reenie, I'll work." And sometimes getting her to the set was a major difficulty. She did not like working. Period.

"I'm not going today," she'd say. "Call 'em up. Tell 'em anything."

"You've got to be kidding, lady. You know you got to go. Why do you do this?"

"I'm not going. Tell 'em anything."

"Okay, if you don't go, I'm going to sing." And then she'd get up, because she knew I was a lousy singer. We played games like that. Once she got there, she would act as if there was no place she'd rather be. I could have socked her. . . . But my God, sometimes to get her there. . . .

We just had codes for everything, especially people, so we could talk all day and nobody would know who we were talking about. Barbara Stanwyck, we'd call her Short Lips. Hugh O'Brian we referred to as Tight-Ass. Robert Taylor was Mr. Clark; Fred MacMurray, Mr. Gordon. One actor we called Snowflakes. We had a director we called Cornflakes. We called Deborah Kerr Miss Continuation because her voice never changed from one film to the other. I won't tell you the name we had for Elizabeth Taylor because she was a very sweet girl and we loved her very much. Miss G. was an extremely funny person. She should have been a comedian. She could get fun out of the darnedest things, and would nearly kill herself laughing. And she loved getting back at people. When she and Eileen, her secretary, were in Africa for *Mogambo,* they wanted to go to this club that was right across the street from the hotel. But the club didn't want any actresses, especially without an escort, so they kept saying they were filled up.

Finally, she said, "Eileen, why don't you call and tell them that you are Clark Gable's secretary and that Mr. Gable is coming in out of the bush and he would like a table for about twenty-four people." Then she and Eileen sat by the hotel window and they watched the waiters hustling to set the tables up. Of course, Clark Gable had no idea; he didn't know anything about it. She laughed about it for years. She'd say, "That's a just reward."

—MEARENE JORDAN

"A mere friend will agree with you, but a real friend will argue."

—Russian Proverb

chick star chart
(or how to the find your sister sign!)

Ever wonder why all your friends' birthdays seem to be clustered in the same month? Perhaps more of us should follow Nancy Reagan's lead and consult the stars! Turns out that some astrological sign pairings can make highly combustible friendships, while others are just heavenly!

Aries: March 21–April 20
Why you're a chick's chick: You're adventurous, confident, and enthusiastic.
Tried and true girlfriends tend to be: Leo, Sagittarius, Taurus
You love her, you hate her: Virgo, Scorpio
She'll make off with your favorite sweater and your boyfriend too: Cancer, Libra, Capricorn, Aries

Taurus: April 21–May 20
Why you're a chick's chick: You are patient, warmhearted, and reliable.
Tried and true girlfriends tend to be: Virgo, Capricorn, Gemini
You love her, you hate her: Libra, Sagittarius
Your "Uh-oh, head for the hills" girlfriend: Aquarius, Leo, Scorpio

Gemini: May 21–June 20
Why you're a chick's chick: You are adaptable, communicative, and witty.
Tried and true girlfriends tend to be: Libra, Aquarius, Gemini
You love her, you hate her: Scorpio, Capricorn
You're oil, she's water: Virgo, Sagittarius, Pisces

Cancer: June 21–July 20
Why you're a chick's chick: You are loving, imaginative, and sympathetic.
Tried and true girlfriends tend to be: Scorpio, Pisces, Virgo
You love her, you hate her: Sagittarius, Aquarius
Your very own Cruella DeVille: Libra, Capricorn, Aries, Cancer

Leo: July 21–August 20
Why you're a chick's chick: You are generous, creative, and faithful.
Tried and true girlfriends tend to be: Sagittarius, Aries, Virgo
You love her, you hate her: Capricorn, Pisces, Leo
Check her ID at the door and then slam it shut: Scorpio, Aquarius, Taurus

Virgo: August 21–September 20
Why you're a chick's chick: You are modest, reliable, and practical.
Tried and true girlfriends tend to be: Capricorn, Taurus, Virgo, Cancer
You love her, you hate her: Aquarius, Aries
Turn your critical eye on these gals: Sagittarius, Pisces, Gemini

Libra: September 21–October 20
Why you're a chick's chick: You are diplomatic, urbane, and sociable.
Tried and true girlfriends tend to be: Pisces, Taurus
You love her, you hate her: Aquarius, Gemini, Libra
Detestation at first sight: Capricorn, Aries, Cancer

Scorpio: October 21–November 20
Why you're a chick's chick: You are determined, intuitive, and magnetic.
Tried and true girlfriends tend to be: Pisces, Cancer, Sagittarius
You love her, you hate her: Aries, Gemini
Turn off your magnetic powers and repel: Aquarius, Taurus, Leo, Scorpio

Sagittarius: November 21–December 20
Why you're a chick's chick: Optimistic, freedom-loving, and honest.
Tried and true girlfriends tend to be: Aries, Leo, Capricorn
You love her, you hate her: Taurus, Cancer, Sagittarius
She's like fingernails on your chalkboard: Pisces, Gemini, Virgo

Capricorn: December 21–January 20
Why you're a chick's chick: You are patient, careful, and humorous.
Tried and true girlfriends tend to be: Taurus, Virgo, Aquarius

(Capricorn continued)
You love her, you hate her: Gemini, Leo, Capricorn
You'll be putting out her fires as she's starting some for you: Aries, Cancer, Libra

Aquarius: January 21–February 20
Why you're a chick's chick: You are honest, original, and loyal.
Tried and true girlfriends tend to be: Gemini, Libra, Aquarius
You love her, you hate her: Cancer, Virgo
She's a combination of your mother in a bad mood and your ex on steroids: Taurus, Leo, Scorpio

Pisces: February 21–March 20
Why you're a chick's chick: You are compassionate, kind, and selfless.
Tried and true girlfriends tend to be: Cancer, Scorpio, Pisces
You love her, you hate her: Leo, Libra
Let this one slither back under her rock: Gemini, Virgo, Sagittarius

Too mAny cowboys

The Shady Ladies of the Central City Motherlode is a group of women, now in its eighth year, that exists to promote the history of a little mining (now gaming) town called Central City, Colorado, and to promote the history of women in the West. We named our group after an annual event in Central City called "Lou Bunch Day" that "honors" shady ladies, aka prostitutes, of the Victorian era.

In our third year together, after winning a few minor awards in parades, we prepared like Olympians for the coming season. We discovered that our best presentations were those when all our members dressed in a theme. So we chose "My Fair Shady Lady," as our theme and each of us dressed Victorian-style in black and white (à la the Ascot horse race scene in *My Fair Lady*) accented with our signature color, hot pink. No two outfits were alike, and the results were stunning. We rented a white carriage with two seats. I think we had fifteen members at the time, and we squeezed ladies in on every possible spot, surely violating some rule of the road—or carriage rental! We had ladies up with the driver, standing on the steps, even sitting on the back of the forward-facing seat. But, oh, did we make a fabulous presentation.

We collected our trophies and ribbons from all over the region as we made a sweep of most of the top awards that year, including Cheyenne Frontier Days—the "Granddaddy of 'em all," as their organizers bill it—in Cheyenne, Wyoming. There are four parades in the week and one award given in each. Our prize was extra special, because it was the festival's 100th anniversary!

The next year the thought on everyone's mind was whether it was possible to win in Cheyenne again. We decided to dress all in

The Shady Ladies in all their glory.

yellow, in accordance with an ordinance that had been proposed for Denver in the late 1800s but was never put into effect. This ordinance stated that ladies of the evening were to wear yellow as a badge of their profession. The story goes that the madams and the feminists banded together and dressed from head to toe in yellow the day the mandate was to take effect. The ordinance was laughed off the books.

I must say we looked fantastic in our bright yellow costumes, again, with no two outfits alike. We rigged an old black iron bed up on a flatbed trailer, tying it down with ratchet straps and bungee cords disguised with strategically placed bouquets of silk sunflowers. We made a yellow bedspread and threaded garlands of sunflowers through the bars on the head and foot of the bed with big yellow bows at the corners.

"Too much of a good thing can be wonderful."—Mae West

We positioned our lightest (youngest) member on the bed and let one lightweight costumed husband climb in next to her for effect. We'd noticed on earlier excursions that the bed was made of cheap metal, and the bars supporting the mattress were showing signs of wear. The other fourteen women had strict instructions to stay off the bed because of its instability. We started down the parade route, everyone trying to find a handhold for the inevitable stops and starts. We were soon caught up in the cheers of the crowd and whooped with wild abandon at each turn. When we reached the end of the parade and learned we had again won, we eagerly accepted a ribbon that was the size of a pizza pan.

In the throes of victory, we threw all caution to the wind when a posse of good-looking cowboys dressed in matching red Western tuxedo shirts hopped on the bed, pulling all of us onto it with them. Holding the ribbon aloft, we squealed with delight and continued on our victory ride through the streets. Suddenly, the woman at the wheel of the truck popped the clutch, the bed lurched forward and back, and, with a bang, fell flat. By that time there were about twenty-five bodies on the bed intertwined in a most immodest way, with arms and legs akimbo.

Some of our ladies were bruised and scraped in the ensuing melee, but fortunately no one was seriously hurt. Now, several years later, the story of "too many cowboys in the bed" is legendary.

—JOAN HEMM, PRESIDENT AND FOUNDER OF THE SHADY LADIES OF THE CENTRAL CITY MOTHERLODE

Clea*n*ing *h*Ouse

In 1967, I lived in a row house in San Francisco. At dawn men headed for work in streetcars that rattled windows. "It's a good place to raise kids," my neighbor Ingrid used to say.

I met Ingrid shortly after moving into the neighborhood. I was attracted to her outspoken manner and to her loud, hoarse voice that seemed to echo through the streets. I was the mouse to her lion. We clinched our friendship when I told her my husband wouldn't let me work. Well, she invited herself in at dinnertime, and standing over him with one hand in her apron pocket and one hand shaking her finger, lectured him about the value of letting me out of the house to work as a maid with her at the hotel next door. "After all, the kids are in school, and she will be getting $19.23 a week!" She sold him on the idea and sold me on her as friend for life. As we knocked on each door, we'd sing out "Room service!" Except at Room 6.

They had the "Do Not Disturb" sign up all the time, so we never went in. In the beginning no one knew they were drug pushers. I was working the front desk when the two of them checked in, a tall skinny man with bulging eyes and long straggly hair and a plain woman.

"You visiting San Francisco for the first time?" I asked.

"Yes," said one.

"No," said the other.

Tony the manager hid in the doorway, shaking his head violently.

I thought he meant I shouldn't ask personal questions.

The next day, trashy folks gathered around Room 6. Cars pulled up, stopping in the middle of the street, radios blasting and holding up the streetcar. "The least they could do is pull their cars into a driveway so the streetcar can pass," Ingrid shouted into the phone. She lived directly across the street from me, and we looked at one another through our kitchen windows as we spoke. "I counted twenty people over there this morning."

One morning, Ingrid and I were cleaning Room 5 when Ingrid realized she could hear the tenants in Room 6. Ingrid was rubbing the mirror clean, and I was damp mopping, slapping the floor.

"Shhh," Ingrid hissed at me.

"What do you mean shhh!" I snapped back.

An agitated Ingrid threw her left hand up and shook it at the wall and with the other hand pressed her finger to her lips. Then I heard it. We both stood with eyes wide, mouths agape, plastered as close to the wall as nature would allow. Words like *snow* and *weed* crept into the conversation we heard.

Later, we joined Tony in the kitchen behind the office for some weak coffee. Ingrid told him what we had heard. I was feeling a little hysterical and shaky. Suddenly we heard the pounding of growing feet.

"Mom, Mom, those guys got guns!" one of our children shouted as they all barged in through the kitchen door.

"Yeah," shouted another soprano voice. "They got guns on, on, on their belts."

"Who?" the adults chorused.

"The men in Room 6," a child said, then asked for a glass of milk.

This only made us more afraid—both Ingrid and I were terrified that our children would be lured into the underground of glassy-eyed people. Something had to be done. But what? Guns added fear. We began to walk our children to and from school and kept them indoors or in their own yards. We had no rest. Needless to say, everyone was getting on everyone else's nerves. Eventually, the two of us decided that something *had* to be done.

Ingrid and I called the police. Two cops came and stood ears to the wall. The two left the room tugging at their belts and adjusting their hats.

"You *must* arrest them!" we said.

"Well, . . ." said one.

Shelley Winters and Constance Dowling were fast friends from the moment they met at the New Theatre School in New York. The two wannabe starlets laughed and cried their way up and down Broadway, supporting and consoling each other through auditions, acting classes, and their relentless pursuit of any job that connected them to the theater. On that road to stardom, Connie landed a job as a Copa Girl, and Shelley decided to give it a shot as well. In her autobiography, *Shelley Also Known as Shirley*, she writes, "I had gone to audition with my elastic beauty-contest bathing suit, complete with powder puffs. They asked me to do a time step, a shuffle-off-to-Buffalo, and two more time steps in double rhythm. I tried, but stumbled and fell. The boss, Signor Perona, a well-known Broadway character, said in Neapolitan, which he didn't think I'd understand, 'This one is crazy and has two left feet.' I shot back, '*Non mi frega niente, Signor Stupido.* (I don't give a [bleep], Mr. Stupid.)'" Thank goodness for Connie, who quickly hustled her out of the theater before any of them got past the shocked realization that Shelley understood Neopolitan—perfectly. Now that's a dance step every good girlfriend has to know.

"Well, what?" Ingrid replied, taking a deep breath.

"Well ma' am, I'm afraid there is nothing we can do!"

"What do you mean? You heard them, they're drug pushers."

"Perhaps they're making this whole thing up 'cause they're writing a book," said the other. "The best thing to do is to have the manager evict them." We were stunned.

A rage welled up in both of us. We marched to the office.

"You have to evict these criminals," we shouted at Tony.

"No way," he said. "They've got guns, remember?"

"Then we will," said Ingrid, grabbing my arm.

I can still feel my feet hitting the floor down the long hallway and wondering if I couldn't just run—persuade my husband to move us to another city, another state. . . .

Ingrid pounded detergent-reddened fists on the door and in a loud voice shouted, "Hey, open the door." The door opened, and I moved away, sure as sin that we'd be wiped out by gunfire.

"Yes?" a gentle woman's voice said.

"This room was reserved. You must leave tomorrow."

"Hold on," the women said. Ingrid was beyond fear. I was frozen to the carpet, plotting my escape. "Okay, fine, we'll be out by tomorrow," the woman said. And they were. Just like that.

I've moved on, but Ingrid still lives there in her drug-free neighborhood.

—LINDA-MARIE

Bo*n* v*O*yage

"O ur ship's come in," I said to Annie, hanging up the phone in our studio apartment, a smaller version of our old dorm room. "Larry's got us a free week on the *Oceanic Independence.*"

"Free?" Annie had no faith in Larry, a sometime boyfriend of mine who worked on a ship that cruised the Hawaiian Islands. Annie and I had met in Philosophy 101. We enjoyed discussing the meaning and purpose of life, but our actual practice of it was limited. In lockstep we had gone from high school to college, college to work.

"Okay, there's probably a catch. But . . ."

Annie and I were preschool teachers with a week's vacation and zero disposable income. Her parents donated their frequent flyer miles, and we flew from San Francisco to Honolulu. Larry met us at the dock. He told us to wait for his signal to board.

All day we watched baggage-laden people boarding ship. We heard the ship's orchestra playing on the upper deck. We saw friends shouting, "Bon voyage!" Just before sunset, the passenger gangway swung majestically away from the ship. Larry appeared by a miniscule opening at the stern, where a paltry gangway still clung on. "Run!" he yelled. We did.

Larry led us through a maze of corridors to a coffin-sized room. His. He worked nights, he explained, so we could alternate in his bunk. Larry outlined the rules for stowaways. Since we didn't have official room keys, certain things were taboo. No leaving the ship when it docked at an island. No sit-down dinners. No excessive hanging out at the buffet. Grinning, Larry wished us luck and told us to have fun.

As night came on, Annie and I huddled together. The ship, plowing through heavy seas, constantly shifted its weight—forward to back, side to side, up and down. The world seemed off its axis.

"Are we stowaways?" Annie asked.

"We're not preschool teachers anymore, that's for sure."

"Have you ever done anything like this before?"

"I've always been too scared."

"What I'm feeling is either existential terror or," Annie paused, "indigestion from the food we ate on the plane."

I laughed. Annie could carve a joke out of any situation.

The next morning, up on deck, the sun hit us like a spotlight. Dressed in jeans and T-shirts and winter pallor, we stood out in a sea of brown, leathery-skinned middle-aged people in swimsuits.

"Food," Annie whispered, pointing to a buffet table, naked hunger in her stare. I felt a little giddy myself. But we were afraid to risk it.

"You're so like my nieces," a woman's voice trumpeted from behind us. Golden tan and golden jewelry, golden hair and golden swimsuit. "Worried about the sun on your skin. Thin as rails. But you must eat." Hooking our arms in hers, Myrna led us to the coffee, Danish, and tropical fruit. Afterward, the three of us sprawled on deck chairs and watched paradise passing.

Myrna stayed with us all day. Between stops at the buffet, we swam in the pool and worked on our tans.

"Don't make friends with the passengers," Larry warned that night. "You can't trust 'em."

Myrna was waiting for us next morning. The three of us were playing shuffleboard when two men in ship uniforms came up to her. "Can we see your passenger key?" one asked.

Annie and I lost our tans in a heartbeat.

"Funny you should ask, officer," Myrna said, smiling brilliantly. "I don't have one."

Feeling like rats deserting a shipmate, Annie and I inched away. The men ushered Myrna off to security. As she rounded a corner of the deck, she looked

taking the plunge

The Grammy-winning, CMA award-carrying Dixie Chicks are known for more than their stellar musical talents—the trio of attitude-packing gals never misses an opportunity to succumb to their rambunctious natures.

The threesome, Emily Robison, Natalie Maines, and Martie Seidel are famous for their goofy sense of humor and ability to laugh at themselves (and each other). When the youngest chick, Emily, married her sweetheart Charlie Robison in Big Bend, Texas, the affair began with Martha Stewart-inspired perfection—prim, polite, and reverent. But with a burst of Dixie Chick spontaneity, Natalie and Martie turned the party on its heel. The sassy instigators convinced all the other bridesmaids to jump into the jacuzzi—dresses and all. The night ended with more guests wet than dry as folks dove into the pool and jumped into the hot tub. What else would you expect at a Dixie Chick wedding? According to Emily, "When your bridesmaids end up in the jacuzzi with their dresses on, it's a good party."

back. Raising a cocky eyebrow, she gave us a broad wink.

An hour later, the ship hooted its departure from the island we'd been docked at. Annie and I watched from the railing, feeling mildly depressed. Then we saw Myrna, dazzling in a chartreuse sarong, an orchid tucked behind her ear, waving to us from the dock. "Bon voyage!" she shouted.

"Captain's checking for stowaways," Larry announced next morning. "You're gonna have to hide."

Panic seized us. We followed Larry deep into the hold. He opened a hatch to a small crawl space. "I'll be back for you when it's safe."

There in the dark, terrorized by the clanging and groaning of the ship's internal organs, we knew what we had to do. Without a word, we climbed out, heads held high and dignity intact. Up, up to the sunlight we climbed, where we promptly headed for the wine and cheese table.

"To Myrna," Annie said, tossing back a wedge of runny Brie on sourdough.

"To Myrna," I replied, saluting her with a glass of perfectly chilled Chardonnay.

—MEREDYTHE CRAWFORD

quick, i need to be another chick

Every gal needs a pseudonym handy—just in case. Whether you're stowing away on a cruise ship or have gotten a little too cozy with the bartender, leave them with an audacious alias and a bogus phone number. Now go out and party like no one knows your name.

your exotic dancer name

To come up with this sexy moniker, replace your first name with the name of your first pet and your last name with your mother's maiden name. For example: Fluffy Nichols, Shortie Quick, Candy Hicks.

your catholic schoolgirl name

Take on your grandmother's first name combined with the name of your favorite Irish pub: Ellen Shenanigan, Catherine O'Brien, Beatrice Benigan.

your southern belle name

Pick your favorite flower and finish it with the surname of the first Civil War figure or *Gone with the Wind* character that comes to mind: Magnolia Lee, Lily Butler, Gardenia Jackson.

your party girl name

Commandeer a favorite comic book character's name and pair it with your libation of choice: Betty Margarita, Cathy Corona, Veronica Cosmopolitan.

your blueblood name

Slip into the name of your favorite soap opera diva plus your designer perfume of choice: Erica Chanel, Laura Shalimar, Lucy Dior.

your "flirty as you wanna be" name

Latch onto your favorite lingerie designer or brand and finish with the last name of your schoolgirl heartthrob: Victoria Cassidy, Frederique Presley, Olga Gibb.

your "good ol'girl" name

Get sentimental and recall your childhood nickname and pair that with your favorite junk food snack: Tiny Hoho, Skeeter Cheeto, Peanut Twinkie.

"A good friend remembers what we were and sees what we can be."

—Janette Oke

the Million-dOllar merMaid

We all get by with a little help from our girlfriends, but we also know the special place allies hold in the workplace. Take the case of Esther Williams and Flossie Hackett. We know Esther as the drop-dead-gorgeous star of the '40s and '50s who swam her way into the hearts of moviegoers in films like *Bathing Beauty* and *Neptune's Daughter,* but few know the name Flossie Hackett. But when your wardrobe consists of minimal fabric, maximum exposure, and thousands of gallons of water, your wardrobe woman is indeed your best friend, and Flossie was the woman behind the scenes ensuring Esther looked great and didn't catch pneumonia between takes.

For one of the aquatic spectaculars, a designer had the idea of creating a swimsuit made from thick red-and-black plaid. While it looked great, it functioned horribly. Esther jumped in the pool and found herself sinking straight to the bottom since she was essentially wrapped in a sponge. Bordering on panic, Esther managed to unzip the saturated suit and swim to the side.

But that was only the beginning of her problems. The set happened to be packed with tourists that day, and there was Esther, buck naked in the water. The star crossed her arms to cover her body as much as possible and whispered, "Flossie. . . ." Flossie, who loved to chide Esther, said, "You silly girl, what did you do? You're totally nude."

"Flossie this is no joke. That suit was too heavy. It had to go! I had to take it off." Flossie scolded her, saying that the suit was expensive and that Esther must dive down and recover it. Finally they got a stagehand to snag the troublesome suit with a skimmer and figured a way to get Esther out of the pool with minimal embarrassment. Flossie got a big towel and cut a circle in it poncho-style, and Esther emerged to appreciative applause from the film crew and onlookers.

Flossie went on to save Esther from more than embarrassment over the years. On the set of *The Million Dollar Mermaid,* Esther, wearing a diver's bodysuit made of 50,000 gold sequins and a gold turban topped with a crown, had to dive from a six-story hydraulic lift into a pool. (And we thought bikinis were daunting.) The crown was so rigid that it snapped Esther's neck as she dove into the water. The director, unaware that she was injured, called it a wrap and dismissed everyone for lunch. In seconds, the entire set was empty, and Esther was still in the pool with a serious neck injury. Thankfully, Flossie had remained on the set to help Esther with her costume and answered her cry for help.

"C'mon, Esther, you're such a kidder. I want to go to lunch. I'm hungry," Flossie remarked.

"Flossie, I'm really in trouble," Esther managed to say, and Flossie immediately got help. Esther had broken three vertebrae that day and spent the next six months in a cast.

chick flicks

Beaches

Boys on the Side

Dangerous Beauty

Enchanted April

The First Wives' Club

The Grass Harp

Hannah and Her Sisters

How Stella Got Her Groove Back

A League of Their Own

Murial's Wedding

My Best Friend's Wedding

Mystic Pizza

Nine to Five

Sirens

Some Like It Hot

Soul Food

The Spitfire Grill

Steel Magnolias

Thelma and Louise

Waiting to Exhale

The Witches of Eastwick

sOle maTes

I rush home from work, excited that it's Wednesday and "Girls' Night Out." But tonight I'm not worrying about my hair, make-up, or what I'm going to wear. Instead, I throw on shorts, T-shirt, and my running shoes. This is a "Girls Night" run—and it's one I hate to miss. Sometimes four women, sometimes as many as a dozen, form a pack running through the Presidio National Park or along San Francisco Bay. We simply call it our "chick run." While we get the occasional leers, more often, we see other runners eyeing us with wonder. Little do they realize how we've become a part of each other's lives.

I began running one year after I moved from Boston to San Francisco. I wanted to improve my health after watching my cousin, Matt, struggle against the cancer ravaging his body. I was only thirty, but I had a new sense of my own mortality. Because I traveled a lot for my new job and spent much of my free time caring for my cousin, I hadn't met very many people. Therefore, I ran alone, keeping Matt in my mind with each step I took and each hill I climbed. I ran in several local races, jealous of the groups of women who ran together. I'd see them stretch and warm up together, motivating each other by their presence. I wanted that level of camaraderie too. But I didn't know many other runners and thought I was too slow for any group. I resigned myself to being a lone runner.

Soon after, I decided to run a marathon. I'd been running for less than a year and wasn't sure I could actually do it. Then a male friend introduced me to three women who were also training for the same race, and they suggested that we take our long runs together. We scheduled them for Saturday mornings, congregating at Shelly's house.

Nicole, Elise, and Shelly had all run marathons before and knew some great urban courses. They also had some pretty impressive finishing times, which did nothing to ease my nervousness. My anxiety subsided the day I found myself keeping pace with Shelly—far from my usual spot at the back—and realized that **together we were leading the pack.**

We ran to build strength and endurance, not for personal records. We ran as a group, keeping together in a tight pack. On good days, we chatted and soaked up the beautiful California sun; on bad days, we complained as one loud, wet voice. Believe me, nothing can bring a group of people together like running 20 miles through the height of El Niño's wrath—hailstorms, deluges, and high winds.

Our friendship seemed to grow stronger as our distances grew longer. Two hours a week provided ample time to share our hopes, dreams, and worries. Shelly was ready for a career change, uncertain as to what she would find and whether she could do it. Nicole was trying to keep a long-distance relationship going and deciding whether she should go to him or stay here. And Elise had been given the news that running was damaging her knee. This would be her last marathon, and she might have to stop running altogether. We talked about family, friends, work, and the cute men running past; each of us had solutions for everyone else's problems. Almost without noticing it, I became stronger, faster, and ready to run.

Marathon day finally came, as did a final attack of nerves. Was I really ready? I had four strong motivating factors: Matt, my original inspiration, and Shelly, Elise, and Nicole. They believed I could do it. I saw no reason to disagree. I muscled through the miles, one by one.

Everyone was running separate paces, so I was alone for most of the race. As I approached the finish line, however, I saw them standing on the side, wildly ringing a cowbell and cheering me on. I recall Shelly's voice yelling my name as I crossed the line. I'll never forget that feeling—I'd found my group!

The marathon was over, but our friendship keeps us running together. We switched from Saturday mornings to Wednesday evenings; we started pairing our runs with dinners or movies or pedicures. Nicole got engaged and eventually moved to Reno to get married. Shelly is freelancing as a computer software instructor. And Elise continues to run, a bit slower and with a big brace, but she does it. Somewhere along the line, more women joined us—friends and friends of friends, all looking for the same kind of companionship and support. Now there are usually eight of us, our runs varying in pace, distance, and terrain. When it comes down to it, though, not so much has changed. We still head out every week, whatever the weather. We still set goals and train for races. We still talk about relationships, work, and our crazy families, and we still appraise the cute men running past us. We just won't let them join us.

—Margaret Hanrahan

sweet Dreams of You

One girl asked me who I was sleeping with to get on the Opry so fast. It hurt so much that I cried day and night. My husband said, "If you don't quit this crying, I'm gonna take you back to the West Coast and forget it." And he would have.

But that's when I met Patsy [Cline]. She was around twenty-seven, and she'd known plenty of hard times trying to make it. Just after I got to Nashville, she was in a car accident that almost killed her. I was on the *Ernest Tubb Record Shop* radio show they do every Saturday night, and I said, "Patsy has the Number One record, 'I Fall to Pieces,' and she's in the hospital." Patsy heard it and asked her husband, Charlie Dick, to bring me to the hospital. She was all bandaged up. We talked a good while and became close friends right away. From then on, if she had a fight with her husband, she'd call me. If I had a fight with Doolittle, I'd call her.

The main reason we became good friends was we were both struggling. Patsy had gotten cut out of a lot of money on a couple of her hit songs, and now she was in the hospital all banged up. We both felt we wouldn't try to hurt each other.

I guess the other girls didn't know about me and Patsy being friends. They called a party at one of their homes to discuss how to stop me from being on the Opry, and they invited Patsy! There were about six of them, younger ones just coming up. I'm not saying who they were, but they know it themselves. The only thing I will say is that Kitty Wells wasn't one of them. She's always been my idol, and she was on the road at the time. Plus she's too good and religious a person to do what the others did. Anyway, inviting Patsy was their mistake. She called me up and told me what the deal was and said we both should go to that meeting. I said I didn't have anything to wear, and besides the meeting was about me. She said going was the best thing to do. She told me to get my hair done, and she came over to my house with a new outfit she had bought for me and she made me go.

When we got to this house, there were all these Cadillacs belonging to the top women singers in the country. We went in there, and they didn't say a word. That ended their plan. Patsy put the stamp of approval on me, and I never had any problems with them again. In fact, they are all my friends now. But I made a point of it when new girls came along to give 'em all a chance, because I wouldn't treat nobody the way they treated me. If you're good, you're gonna make it.

Patsy and Loretta.

Me and Patsy got closer together all the time. She taught me a lot of things about show business, like how to go on stage and how to get off. She even bought me a lot of clothes. Many times when she bought something for herself,

chicks who rock

she would buy me the same thing. She gave me rhinestones—I thought they were real diamonds, and I still have the dresses she bought me, hanging in my closet. She gave me one pair of panties I wore for three years. They were holier than I am!

She even bought me curtains and drapes for my house because I was too broke to buy them. And she offered to pay me to go on the road with her just to keep her company. She was a great human being and a great friend.

—LORETTA LYNN

"Little gal, no matter what people say or do,
no matter what happens,
you and me are gonna stick together."

—Patsy Cline to Loretta Lynn

That's why tHey cAll it "Panty" Hose

I spotted Lisa in one of my classes during the first week of my college junior year. I was wearing army fatigues—don't you hate your fashion past?—and she was wearing some prissy pink Laura Ashley-type ensemble with accessories galore, headband, and a real purse. Someone obviously forgot to tell her she was in college. Anyway, one day in class, I talked with her and was surprised to learn not only that was she fun to shock, but that she was very down to earth, loyal, and accepting. She also could discuss things such as butt size and acne—two major concerns of any college woman—with a straight face. Or at least with me. And she immediately won me over by sharing her confidence-of-the-decade: she was a virgin and hadn't slept with her boyfriend of four years. Who couldn't respect this woman and her willpower! Our differences kept us intrigued and cemented our friendship, which still exists to this day.

My other buddy, Rebecca, had wild hair like I did. She was Phi Beta Kappa, president of the student body, and a complete type A. She was a very proper, ambitious, smart gal who always did her homework, a modest sort of person all the boys fell in love with. She was also beautiful, athletic, and very private; we never saw Rebecca naked, and that was unusual given our various states of undress while living together.

One weekend, Rebecca and I were invited to a date party. It involved getting on buses that would take us to San Francisco to a bar for dancing and drinking. I had a date, a cute friend of a friend.

Since Lisa was my own personal Emily Post, I relied on her for all questions of social etiquette and fashion. As we—Lisa, Rebecca, and myself—got dressed, me in a black miniskirt, midriff-baring top, heels, and nylons, I noticed major panty lines under my hose and skirt. Lisa explained, very matter-of-fact, that you were not supposed to wear underwear under your panty hose—that was why it had that little cotton patch. Well, that made perfect sense, and so Rebecca and I quickly stripped off our undies.

We got on the chartered bus, rode into the city, and after a few hours at the party, Rebecca and I and our two dates decided to leave the party and roam bars. By this time, I was getting along with my date quite well. It was getting late though, and we were pretty drunk, and Rebecca and I had a momentary sober thought that we should go back to the party. We arrived

the mother of invention

Nineteenth-century girlfriends Amelia Bloomer, Elizabeth Cady Stanton, and Elizabeth Miller are credited with liberating the female form. While traveling with her cousin and women's rights crusader Stanton, Miller quickly tired of dragging around the weighty undergarments of the time. In frustration, she engineered a loose frock of pantaloons paired with a short skirt that replaced the bulky petticoats. The high-profile ladies wore the fashions, word caught on, and voilà—the first *Glamour* Do. Amelia Bloomer, publisher of America's first feminist journal, called *The Lily*, shared the revolutionary garment with her readers, and requests poured in for patterns. The male-dominated mainstream press ridiculed the garments as "Bloomerisms" and christened the freeing garments "bloomers." The rest, shall we say, is herstory.

just as the bus was pulling out, and despite our squealingest efforts, it left without us. We only had about $10 between us, but our dates lived in the city and they invited us to stay at their house. This was sounding pretty satisfactory to me; I didn't want my newfound cute guy to disappear with my buzz.

I ended up sleeping in my party clothes and waking up with the worst pair of snagged and torn panty hose you have ever seen. My friend Rebecca? She was in the same boat. So we decided to ditch the telltale panty hose and leave the premises. There we were, standing on a street corner, walking around in high heels, miniskirts, and *no underwear.* Did I mention it was a breezy day? Or that we ended up taking the train home? We lived everyone's "forgot my underwear" nightmare, and once we got over our embarrassment, we realized that it *was* pretty hysterical.

—Karen Bouris Newton

"I base most of my fashion taste
on what doesn't itch."

—Gilda Radner

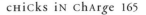

Cowgirls *just* Wanna Have *fun*

I t seems that every time Lynette and I get together we get into just enough trouble to keep things interesting. A dangerous combination of charm, beauty, and attitude, Lynette could be standing at the scene of the crime holding the smoking gun, and the officers would all assume she had been trying to help and that the gun jumped into her hand!

Once, on an overnight getaway, we were driving back to our hotel after dancing all night long in a club called the Rock House, which was full of cowboys. With the stereo cranked, we were gossiping about the men we had danced with. In between laughing and talking we were taking turns belting out our rowdy girls'-night-out theme song, "If It Don't Take Two," by Shania Twain, when a police car's blue lights illuminated our rear view mirror. Unbeknownst to me, Lynette didn't have her driver's license with her or the registration on the car, and her insurance was not current. Oh, and did I mention that she was going 60 in a 45 miles-per-hour zone?

As we sat on the side of the road, three police cruisers found the need to join in on the excitement. I suppose it takes that much manpower to administer a sobriety test to a 5'3", 110-pound blonde. She passed the test, and after chatting with us for more than half an hour the officers simply bid us good night and drove away! No ticket, no warning, no nothing. I was terrified, but Lynette simply laughed and cued up Shania one more time on the CD player.

One night, after sneaking into the Salinas Rodeo, we went where every cowboy and cowgirl go after the rodeo—the Rodeo Inn, the honky-tonk haven of rodeo's elite. It is the locals' chance to rub elbows with greats like Ty Murray, the seven-time world champion cowboy, and Tuff Hedeman, who's immortalized in the movie *Eight Seconds.* As you would expect, at the door to the bar, there was a line that reached halfway down the block.

We had waited about half an hour in line when Tuff Hedeman and Dan Etbauer, two of rodeo's most famous and adored, walked right up next to us! They knew someone in line ahead of us and struck up a conversation that we quickly eavesdropped our way into. Just about that time, I saw someone I knew leaving the bar, and he let me have his wristband, required for getting into the club. He only had one, so Lynette would have to stand in line. But she was not too unhappy about that, considering the stellar company she was in. I told her where I would meet her inside and started to walk off. As about fifteen little girls came running up and begged for Tuff's autograph, he turned and drawled to me, "Where are you going, darlin'? You are just going to leave me out here in the cold?" he asked. I smiled big and replied, "I guess that I am. Nice meeting you." And with that, I walked inside. Lynette said later she wished I could have seen his amazed face!

—JANNA ROBERTSON

It's a snap for wOmen f Action and AdVenture

He's all mine!"

"I saw him first."

Snap. Click. Another one for the scrapbook. We were four girlfriends with cameras going for a day hike in Yosemite National Park. Our goal was to photograph the spectacular beauty of the local flora and fauna, but we got a little distracted by another sort of wildlife. . .

Karen, Renee, Theresa, and I started at the lookout point where tourists routinely gather for the obligatory photo of Half Dome. That's when Theresa got things rolling. She noticed a foreign tourist taking a photo of his friend, and instead of making the usual friendly offer to take a photo of the two of them, she sidled up to the befuddled man, draped her arm around his shoulders, flashed a bright smile, and offered to be in the picture with him. We all laughed, and the men were delighted.

Calling ourselves "Women of Action and Adventure," we are a competitive group by nature and seize wild, wacky moments whenever we can. Not to be outdone by Theresa's bold act, we turned the day into a no-holds-barred contest to see which of us could get our picture taken with the most men. The loosely constructed rule was that once a man was in a photo with one of us, he

Sherry's winning shot.

couldn't be counted if any of the rest of us got one with him, too. So we had to be nimble and outwit each other as we hiked together. We also had to cooperate since we couldn't take the pictures by ourselves.

The results were fabulous! Among our favorite snapshots are pictures of one of us with the head chef at The Ahwanee lodge, our park bus driver, a retired man visiting the park with his mortified twelve-year-old grandson, a hot dog stand vendor, the waiter at a bar, a flattered trash collector, and fellow hikers. Karen upped the ante when we stopped for gas. Jumping out of the car, she quickly got all of the station attendants to be photographed with her. My finest moment was when I asked a park ranger to be photographed with me—a coup since he was in uniform!

It was grand fun and a lifetime memory that boosted our self-esteem as well as that of all the men we encountered. And I have the pictures to prove it!

—SHERRY WICKWIRE

"All serious daring starts from within."

—Harriet Beecher Stowe

About the Editors

Ame Mahler Beanland is an award-winning editor and art director. Co-author of *Mother's Nature,* she has contributed to numerous other books on topics ranging from women's history to gardening. Ame lives in northern California with her husband.

Emily Miles Terry is a marketing and publicity consultant for book publishers. As the publicist for the bestselling Wild Women series, she grew to have a great affinity for untamed tales. Currently she lives in Boston with her husband and two children.

AcknOwledgMents

Boundless gratitude to all the chicks who shared their adventures with us. Your generous spirit and sassy wit inspired us and made this more fun than work. Chick cheers to Brenda Knight for your relentless insistence that we "write a book about friendship." To our editor Mary Jane Ryan, thank you for helping us weave this all together. To the super-talented and hyper-fun Martha Newton Furman, thank you for creating the fabulous illustrations for the book. To Jody Fidler for her expert legal advice. To the chicks and guys at Conari Press who lent their support and patience with the endless supply of pink stuff we produced on a daily basis: Suzanne Albertson, Leslie Berriman, Jenny Collins, Sharon Donovan, Will Glennon, Mignon Freeman, Everton Lopez, Heather McArthur, Lynn Meinhardt, Rosie Levy, Leah Russell, Claudia Smelser, and Pam Suwinsky. — AMB and EMT

To my partner in crime, Emily, thank you for all the silly conversations, your constant friendship, unwavering dedication, and for countering my moments of drama queen desperation with your clear-headed insight. I cherish our friendship. Love to my BFF Kim Nichols and Justina Quick Radcliff—who know all about me and miraculously still want to be my girlfriends. To Gina Larkin, Donna Lord, Marie McEnery, Nancy Milla, and Claudia Sadlon—the best chickmates a girl could ever have. To the ladies of the Chick 'n Chat—thank you for listening to my endless chick chatter. To Leigh Bordelon and Susan Jones, I would have wasted away without our chick power lunches. To the book-loving ladies at Towne Center Books who were so generous with their time. Special gratitude to my gal pals

Andrea Adams, Celia Berg, Tammy Knight, and Kelli Wright for countless good times. For my mother, Mary "Bootsie" Mahler, who taught me all about friendship and that life is too short to take yourself so damn seriously. To Aunt Detrice for inspiration and boundless joy. For my sister Kathy Robertson, who keeps me out of serious trouble. Thank you to Bill Kastigar who was not afraid to connect with his inner chick and suggest the title for the book. And most importantly, to the one person this chick can't live without—Peter Beanland. Thank you for joining in the girlfriend banter and not only enduring, but enjoying, all the chickfests. — A M B

To "superstar" Ame, without whose diligence, inspiration, and brilliance this book would never have existed. For all those fortunate enough to know her, Ame is the true embodiment of the word *friend*. For my mother, Karen, who taught me how to find and keep good friends. To my grandmothers, Emily and Hazel, whose model of elegance and dignity have kept me on the right track (most of the time). To the very special Fun Bunch—Amy, Elisabeth, Jill, Jody, Kim, Terry, and Tracy—for being there. To great girlfriends Jill Bauer, Kristen Bush, Karen Bouris, Catherine Patience, and Leslie Rossman, who have made me laugh, and laugh, and laugh over the years. To Stephanie (Tippie), my first tried and true buddy. To my father, Tom, and brother, John, for putting up with my never-ending chick chats and phone hogging as a teen. To my grandfather, Hans, for letting me barrage him with books. To Mary, for getting me going with the Blue Nail Polish story. And to my one and only, Dave, for endless love and support, and my precious Julia and Henry (you aren't allowed to read this book until you both graduate from high-school) wishing you years of wonderful friendships and tremendous fun with your buddies. — E M J

CrediTs

Joan Hemm is the president and founder of the Shady Ladies of the Central City Motherlode, Inc., a volunteer, nonprofit, educational organization that exists to promote the history of a little mining (now gaming) town called Central City in Colorado, and to promote the history of women in the west.

Ilana Singer, Professor of C-CTherapy®, Director of Women's Division, is a licensed psychotherapist in the human behavior field since 1972. Co-owner of the Center for Counter-Conditioning Therapy® in Oakland, California, she established the Women's Division in 1985. As a clinical ethnologist, she teaches patients emotional self-management skills. Besides autobiographical pieces, she is the author of clinical monographs posted at the Center's Web site *www.c-ctherapy.org* and the author of the forthcoming book *Emotional Recovery After Natural Disasters: How to Get Back to Normal Life.*

SuzAnne C. Cole taught English for more than twenty years at Houston Community College before retiring in 1996 to concentrate on writing. Her essays have been published in *Newsweek* ("My Turn," June 22, 1998), the *Houston Chronicle,* the *San Antonio Express-News,* and *Personal Journaling* (October 1999). She is the author of *To Our Heart's Content: Meditations for Women Turning 50* (Contemporary, 1997) as well as numerous works of poetry and fiction in literary magazines and anthologies.

Permissions to reprint previously published materials:

"The Dance Class" reprinted by permission of SuzAnne C. Cole ©1999. Originally published in *Troika*, Issue 22, Fall 1999 • "A Royal Adventure" reprinted with the permission of Simon and Schuster from *Sarah Duchess of York: My Story* by the Duchess of York. © 1996 by the Duchess of York. • "Hell's Belles" reprinted by permission of HarperCollins Publishers, Inc. from *Dolly: My Life and Other Unfinished Business* by Dolly Parton. ©1994 by Dolly Parton. • "The Sweet Potato Queens" from *The Sweet Potato Queens' Book of Love* by Jill Conner Browne. © 1999 by Jill Conner Browne. Reprinted by permission of Three Rivers Press, a division of Random House, Inc. • "Sweet Dreams of You" from *Loretta Lynn: Coal Miner's Daughter* ©1976 by Henry Regnery Publishing. All rights reserved. Reprinted by special permission of Regnery Publishing, Inc. Washington, D.C. • "Capricious Capricorns" excerpted from *Ava: My Story*, reprinted with permission of Thorndike Press, ©1994 Ava Gardner. • "Bean Hollow Beach Day" reprinted by permission of Ilana Girard Singer © 1991. First published in *Coping Magazine*, Summer 1991 under the title "Survivor's Story."

photo credits:
All photos that accompany the stories are courtesy of the authors. Photos on page 173: Ame Mahler Beanland by Susan Jones of Way Past My Bedtime Productions; Emily Miles Terry by Dave Terry.

Index

W

Weller, Frances Ward, 73
Wells, Rebecca, xv, 7
West, Mae, 92, 144
Wickwire, Sherry, 168–169
Williams, Esther, 155–156
Winters, Shelley, 147

Y

Yakhlef, Cilicia A., 30–34
"Your Roommate's a Hawg," 18–20

Z

"Zen and Destruction," 64–67

2 Be books

2 Be Books is a two-chick company—Ame and Emily—and you've just read our first book. We hope you enjoyed it (yea) or perhaps you didn't like it (bummer). Since we are creating many more books, we'd truly value your feedback—good or bad. Our hope is to produce books that will make you laugh—that spontaneous, loud and embarrassing type of laugh. Or perhaps they'll make you think and move you to reach out to someone, or reach into yourself. If you want to learn more about us or share your opinions, please contact us. You can visit our web sites:

www.itsachickthing.net *or* www.2bebooks.com

Or you can "chick chat" with us via e-mail at: 2bebooks@home.com or by writing us at:

2 Be Books
P.O. Box 1562
Jamaica Plain, MA 02130

"My home is where my books are."

—Ellen Thompson

tHe end

Thank you for reading our book.

AMB & EMT